WHAT HAPPENS IN MY GARDEN

Books by Louise Beebe Wilder

The Fragrant Path
Adventures with Hardy Bulbs
Color in Your Garden
What Happens in My Garden

What Happens in My Garden

By Louise Beebe Wilder

Foreword by
Elisabeth Sheldon

Collier Books
Macmillan Publishing Company
New York

Collier Macmillan Canada
Toronto

Maxwell Macmillan International
New York Oxford Singapore Sydney

Collier Books
Macmillan Publishing Company
866 Third Avenue, New York, NY 10022

Collier Macmillan Canada, Inc.
1200 Eglinton Avenue East, Suite 200
Don Mills, Ontario M3C 3N1

Library of Congress Cataloging-in-Publication Data

Wilder, Louise Beebe, 1878–1938.
    What happens in my garden / by Louise Beebe Wilder ;
foreword by Elisabeth Sheldon.
        p.   cm.
    Reprint. Originally published: New York : Macmillan,
1935.
    Includes index.
    ISBN 0-02-040841-2
    1. Flower gardening—United States. 2. Flowers—
United States. 3. Rock gardens—United States. I. Title.
SB405.W716   1991   90-19331   CIP
635.9—dc20

Macmillan books are available at special discounts for bulk
purchases for sales promotions, premiums, fund-raising, or edu-
cational use. For details, contact:

Special Sales Director
Macmillan Publishing Company
866 Third Avenue
New York, NY 10022

First Collier Books Edition 1991

10 9 8 7 6 5 4 3 2 1

Printed in the United States of America

CONTENTS

[v]

FOREWORD

THOSE of us who have been combing second-hand bookstores looking for the works of Louise Beebe Wilder are extremely gratified to see them coming back into print at last. Considering that countless *new* garden books are being launched these days, it is a testimonial to the real value of Mrs. Wilder's works that they should be reprinted to compete, as they must, with the latest how-to horticultural books and all those sumptuous coffee-table productions full of gorgeous photographs. It is also a testimonial to the conviction of the publishers that there are enough real gardeners in this country, people who work with and delight in reading about plants, to make it worth their while to reprint them. I'm sure the venture will succeed, for although she uses the language and the botanical nomenclature of her time (which hasn't changed enough to make for confusion), Mrs. Wilder's vast knowledge of plants and their ways, her close association with and observation of them, and her clear, beautiful, and simple prose style, are just as valuable and appealing to us today as they were to the readers of her time.

In *What Happens in My Garden* there are whole chapters on bulbs, such as allium and snowdrops, and on specific genera, such as *Linum*, *Thymus*, *Silene*, and *Oenothera*, and on creepers for the rock garden. The chapter on rock garden shrubs provides suggestions and descriptions of small shrubs, some of which might well be used in perennial borders or in other planting areas around the house, as well as in rock gardens.

Certainly we can learn from her now. As I reread *What Happens in My Garden*, I found myself taking notes: "See p. 208 for sowing clematis seed . . . p. 174 for white flowers in the border . . . She used a salmon lychnis near purple and lavender iris . . . *Coreopsis rosea* prefers acid bogs" (and I have it on a limey slope. So *that's* why it's not doing well!).

Louise Beebe was born in Baltimore in 1878 and pre-served lovingly her memories of the Maryland country-side when, later, as Mrs. Wilder, she lived and gardened in New York. Over the years she traveled widely, visiting many gardens in other countries, but the two she created for herself were in Pomona, New York, and in what was then rural Bronxville. Apparently the advent of two children didn't slow down her gardening, administrative, and writing activities. She founded the Working Gar-deners Club and became vice-president of the Federated Garden Clubs of New York and editor of its journal, *New York Gardens*. She was also a director and member of the advisory council of the New York Botanical Garden. All this while she was writing nine gardening books as well as many magazine and newspaper articles. In 1937, the year before she died, she was awarded a gold medal for hor-ticultural achievement by the Garden Club of America.

The first of Louise Wilder's books appeared in 1916, but most of them spanned that fruitful period between the two world wars, a time that produced so many good writers—and, apparently, good gardeners.

Foreword

Up until the time I read this book I was under the impression that Americans, with a few notable exceptions, had never gone in much for serious gardening. Of course there had always been wealthy people with gardens—and gardeners—but the others? So it came as something of a shock to hear Mrs. Wilder describing countless plants that she said were "easily available" but which are not to be had for love or money in this country today. It follows that if it was worthwhile for nurserymen to grow them, there must have been lots of people who wanted to buy them—gardening people, people who planned and tended their own gardens for the most part.

After describing eight kinds of hybrid colchicums and fourteen species with their special forms, she says, apologetically, that she's just scratched the surface of the genus; there are many other colchicums in existence, but they're not available in the United States, due to the quarantine, which she mentions often and sorrowfully.

In 1919, due to increasing public alarm over the incidence of insects and diseases on plants coming from abroad, the government placed restrictions on the importation of nursery stock, including plants, seeds, bulbs, and roots, except for experimental purposes. Vegetable and flower seeds were, however, permitted free entry, as well as fruits, cereals, and other plant products imported for food, medicine, and manufacturing purposes. Exceptions were also made for some plants and for bulbs, including those of lilies, narcissus, hyacinths, tulips, and crocuses, which could be brought in with a permit. In 1923, unlimited entry was granted to bulbs of *Chionodoxa*, *Galanthus*, *Scilla*, *Fritillaria*, *Muscari*, *Ixia*, and *Eranthis*. A quarantine was then imposed on narcissus bulbs in 1926 but was revoked in 1935 because it hadn't been effective in controlling the spread of bulb flies and nematodes. In 1930, a long list was published of all bulbs, corms, and tubers (including colchicums, narcissus, and dozens of others) that, if clean, no longer required certification to enter the country. Obviously, the quarantine was not so stringent as one might deduce from Mrs. Wilder's protests—but one can readily understand the feelings of a gardener who has not been accustomed to having any restrictions at all imposed on the purchasing of plants and bulbs from abroad.

Her choice was wide, nevertheless. If we wanted to get those twenty-two colchicums, or some of the *thirty-four* kinds of species iris (most of them American) that she covers in the two iris chapters, we would have to look for seed in seed-exchange lists and try to grow our own. Nursery catalogues now offer half the number of colchicums and, as for iris, they list mostly hybrids of bearded, Japanese, and Siberians. A few fancy nurseries carry *Iris cristata*, perhaps *I. pseudacorus*, several bulb iris, the Japanese *I. tectorum*, and that's all. In the chapter on wild roses suitable for gardens, Mrs. Wilder concentrates especially on native American roses, seven of them, of which she is especially fond. Does anyone sell them now—*Rosa setigera, blanda, arkansana, nitida, lucida*, and the others? Perhaps now that we've rediscovered the pleasures of gardening, small specialty nurseries will spring up again to furnish us with a wider variety of interesting plants.

You will find a lot about rock gardening in this book. It was a pursuit Mrs. Wilder promoted enthusiastically

(Linc Foster called her the doyenne of American rock gardening) and tolerantly, being persuaded that even when the amateur's efforts resulted in a garden that was far from beautiful, the activity itself, the attempt to accommodate, to please and cause to flourish, small plants from the mountains of the world added a wonderful new dimension to lives that might otherwise be very dreary.

It is remarkable, though, that even with her wide knowledge of recherché alpines, Mrs. Wilder puts in a good word for easy rock plants which "seldom receive sufficient credit . . . they ask so little—which, instead of arousing our gratitude seems to engender a faint contempt." She was obviously not one of those gardeners who value only plants that are scarce and skittish.

Nor did she treasure only small plants; in the garden she recounts for us, her Westchester County garden, she grew all manner of perennials, from tiny alpine jewels to six-foot-tall border plants. We are not told anything of the design of the garden but we read of her experience with each plant, what she learned of its needs, and how to site and please it.

It is rare to find an expert in any field who is able to write well on a subject—who can arouse and keep the interest of the layman as well as that of fellow experts. If the expert is able to occasionally amuse, as well as instruct the reader, so much the better—and so much the rarer. *What Happens in My Garden* abounds in felicitous sentences such as these about creeping plants which, as Mrs. Wilder says, "don't stay put":

[A creeper] is a restless creature and advances at varying rates of speed, according to its character and how well it is suited as to soil and situation, in all directions at once, often entering the unguarded preserves of the helpless and choice little rock dwellers that sit tight and stationary, unable to protect themselves, where it smothers and strangles with relentless energy and efficiency.

She says that "these green destroyers are not uncommonly offered in catalogues as desirable rock plants, but they should be avoided as the plague . . . " *Veronica filiformis* is one of these. After describing its beauty, she says it must be put on a bank all by itself as

small plants are not safe in its vicinity. It gobbles them up . . . and then flows as smoothly as a placid green river above their little drowned bodies.

Elsewhere, in speaking of *Daphne genkwa*, she writes:

It is a weakly little bush . . . irregular and seemingly irresolute. Each year I think it has perished, so long do its dark branches remain impassive.

While writing this foreword I found that I had copied that last sentence in a notebook ten years ago. Mrs. Wilder chose her words as meticulously as she chose plants for her garden.

And so we welcome the reappearance of a work by the woman who was, and probably remains, America's best garden writer. It may provide inspiration for writers of garden books today and will be sure to delight those who love both plants and the English language.

Elisabeth Sheldon
July 1990

WHAT HAPPENS IN MY GARDEN

CHAPTER I

ROCK gardening is a fairly recent preoccupation in America, and to judge by the publicity it is receiving, it has taken a mighty hold upon our imaginations. Much is being written for and against it. It has achieved the notoriety of the columnist's columns, and Walter Prichard Eaton, whose counsels are invariably towards perfection, has poked a little fun at its followers, while admitting that with hands torn and roughened from excavating crevices and ramming in soil, he has joined the ranks of these slightly demented ones. Every one, in short, whether particularly concerned with gardening or not, is having something to say about this special phase of it, and most of it is more or less fanatical, one way or the other.

It is the reputedly unromantic and practical Englishman who started us off on this romantic and impractical career. He has himself over a period of many years mastered the technique of rock gardening. He has learned—that is to say, many of the English have—how to bring the mountain with all its magic and mystery, its poetry and fierce wistfulness, and its delightful inhabitants, to the feet of thousands of Mohammeds, and he is unobtrusively teaching the rest of the world to do likewise. There are as yet, however, not

[1]

many persons on this side of the Atlantic (perhaps they may be counted on the fingers of both hands) who know how to build a rock garden that is at once a beautiful scene and a safe and comfortable home for the rarer alpines.

Let me hasten to say that I am not one of these gifted ones. My own rock garden is of the use-what-you-have-and-you-haven't-much variety, but truth compels me to add that an amazing variety of fairly "difficult" plants find it habitable. Nor are our landscape architects as a class among those to be counted off on the ten digits. Many of these talented folk can and often do create something that looks very well, but seldom will anything more chancy than Arabis, Alyssum, or creeping Phlox survive for more than a few seasons in their careful erections. The reason for this is that the landscape architect is not conversant with the little individual, and to him exasperating, wayward ways of the thousand kinds of wild, and too often woolly, plants commonly assembled in a rock garden, and is as yet out of sympathy with the fixed determination of these small individuals to be happy in their own way, or to die in the attempt. To the landscape architect a garden is, or should be, a work of art created by an artist; a rock garden too often appears to him the work of a lunatic, or at very best a person devoid of any knowledge of or feeling for art. Yet it is, strangely enough, this "lunatic's" garden that is often the most satisfactory from the standpoint of the plants.

This is of course not entirely as it should be, nor need we regard it as a permanent state of affairs. It is quite possible to build in almost any situation a rock garden that is at once beautiful, truthful, and efficient if you possess the taste, the vision, and the ingenuity —and too often money must enter in if you are far from proper materials—to create in diminished replica a lovely natural scene, a bit of mountain side, a crag above a pool, a valley winding between projecting cliffs, a bit of jewelled alpine lawn, or the like, the while the scope of your understanding and sympathy runs to the proper care and feeding of each little wilding you have enticed thither and the skill to give it a happy setting. ·But the power to do all this is no common or mean endowment, and is not to be learned in a mere month of Sundays.

Naturally, not all rock gardeners will have the same aim in view. There will always be those who do it because it is at the moment "being done." These scarcely count. Others will delight chiefly in a display of lovely and harmonious color. But the ones who will find the most pleasure in this type of gardening are the serious students of alpine and other wild plants. The gardens of these folk will be chiefly collectors' gardens, devoted in the main to the culture of plants that do not thrive in the level borders, but require special soil conditions, sharp drainage, special care. To this class of gardener the first interest is the *plant,* and while many will strive to give it a beautiful and congruous setting, many others will be satisfied just to provide for it conditions in which it can live happily far from its native habitat.

So far as the right construction and setting of a rock garden go, there is a recently published book that shows us just how to go about it. It is "Natural Rock Garden-

ing," by B. H. B. Symons-Jeune. It is a true counsel
of perfection, and more than likely when you have
studied the many fine and illuminating illustrations and
assimilated its incontrovertible precepts you will go out
and view your own humble congeries of assorted rocks
and what not, garnered from hither and yon, with deep
dejection. Until! Until your straying glance happens
to light upon the way some diffident and captious imp
of a plantling from the high Sierras, the Caucasus, the
Mojave Desert, preens itself and flourishes as if at
home in the surroundings you have made for it with
your bungling hands and with a prayer in your heart.
It is then that your crushed spirit will lift and soar,
and feeling a little like God (or a god of sorts, anyway)
and only slightly chastened by the memory of those
beautiful illustrations, you will go forth and collect
another rock or two from the roadside, or from your
neighbor's wall, and scan the catalogues, seed and plant,
with a renewed sense of power and impending adventure. Study this book, by all means, and you will learn
from it; but do not allow it to turn you from your
purpose or dampen your enthusiasm. For you have
something in your hand which if you hold it will bring
you happiness.

If a large proportion of made-in-America rock gardens still have the appearance of desolate stone heaps
that Nature is half-heartedly trying to cover, I am
firmly of the opinion that for the present this is of no
moment. Now that I have set this down I seem to hear
murmurings from polite circles and mutterings from
less polite circles—or perhaps the reverse. And I must
hasten to add my belief that truth and beauty always

matter tremendously, but at the same time there is good and ample excuse for these imperfect rock gardens. We are not all born full-fledged with wings to fly; we must first flop about and make mistakes and stone-heap "mountains" whose appearance offends the esthetic. But a large proportion of humanity treads a well-beaten path; the common round is more often than not a humdrum one, often weary and anxious and drab. From such conditions—and they are not by any means the portion of the poor alone—a rock garden, whether conceived by a master builder and carried out with consummate skill, or just the best-you-can-do-with-what-you-have-at-hand kind tenderly tended, opens a way of escape, provides the tugging spirit with wings to carry it beyond the rumblings of the Depression, the irk of the too familiar, the cramping circumference of that common round. It is more than beauty—any sincere attempt at growing alpine plants—it is release to seek beauty, which is better by a long shot than finding it done up in a parcel on the doorstep. Perhaps with equal truth this may be said of all sincere gardening, but I believe that no other type of gardening so fully engages all the faculties, so successfully meets all tastes, so nicely fits itself to the scope of all pocketbooks and of all physical resources.

In the London *Morning Post* some years ago I remember that H. A. Tipping asked the question:

"Does the lure of Alpine gardening lie entirely in the inherent grace and beauty of the plants, or does it, in part, arise from the fact that this form of horticulture occupies the least space and the most attention?"

Who can answer this question, and what does the

answer matter? The lure is there, and the reward for patient, intelligent work assured. Never do I drive through the humbler suburbs and note the little front yards upheld by banks studded with stones and planted with rock plants of sorts, nearly always flourishing, without experiencing a sort of exultation. I say to myself that the dweller in that drab little house is more fortunate than his neighbor who spreads a bit of smug lawn or flaunts a row of floor-mop Dahlias. His spirit is one that is not circumscribed by his dwelling or his dull job. He is not conscious of their limitations. He is a citizen of the world. Sentimental? No. Let him stand behind the counter six days a week, or drive the ice cart, or add up interminable rows of figures, there is yet the seventh day when he calls to mind such unbelievable places as Corsica, the Andean slopes, the Himalayas, or feels the free wind blow through dim canyons and across sunlit plains, and in his mind's eye sees heavy snows settle slowly upon wild heights. For you may grow Sweet William and Hollyhocks all your life—and your mother before you—without inquiring whence they originally came, but with alpines it is different. Where they came from is a prime part of the delight and the interest in making their acquaintance.

Jason Hill, an Englishman who has done some of the most delightful writing on gardening (only not enough of it) in our time, wrote this:

"In a rock garden we foster a little patch of the wilderness that stands to us for freedom."

That perhaps is the real secret of the fascination of rock gardening, if we must define its fascination. While working among the little plants of the far places of the world we forget the narrowness of our own orbit; we recapture the freedom we felt on some hill-spent holiday and breathe again the delicious clearness of the ambient air.

Last summer I saw in the *New York Times* a letter from Wayne, Nebraska. It read in part: "In a twenty-by-thirty-foot space in his back yard A. V. Teed is growing ninety varieties of wild flowers collected mostly in Nebraska. Plants from arid lands and from marshes, from mountain sides, woods and plain grown side by side, are aided by soil variations arranged by the gardener." The article gave the further information that Mr. Teed is a member of the faculty of Wayne Normal School. Here, then, is a man who has found a way of escape and of refreshment from one of the most arduous of professions. How reviving to turn from training the more or less calculable, and often disappointing, human mind to the entertainment of those incalculable and enchanting guests he has brought to accept his hospitality!

Many professional people find refreshment in rock gardening; more letters come to me from physicians than from any other class of persons. Teachers come next. They undoubtedly find in its varied problems and intricacies, as well as in the pristine loveliness of the plants they grow, complete diversion from overwhelming responsibilities of devastating monotony and weight.

I could tell much that is significant about the persons who find their way to my garden to discuss their hobby, always with that look in their eyes of seeing things beyond the general ken that is common to rock gardeners, or who write to me from all parts of the country of what it has meant to them personally. Many of these recitals are full of pathos, of courage; they tell of almost insurmountable obstacles overcome, of burdens more easily borne because of one of those little rock piles at which some of us are wont to smile or scoff. It is such testimony that makes me say that even if many of our rock gardens are crude and unbeautiful it is no matter. Each serves a useful purpose. People, more people than you perhaps have any idea of, many of them far from the centers, dwelling on the bleak prairies, in lonely mountain districts, in little isolated towns, who do not belong to garden clubs, who have little money to spend on their pleasure, whose lives hold little gaiety, are getting delight out of them and are finding in them something that they seek— solace from sorrow, from care, an end to boredom, that dread disease, what you will. And they are accomplishing an amazing amount with so little to work with.

And so I reiterate: Enjoy your rock garden whether or no. Let it do for you what it will. And do not worry if it falls short of what you know to be ideal. There is much happiness to be found in a lower atmospheric stratum than that in which swims the particular star to which you have hitched your horticultural chariot.

CHAPTER II

SNOWDROPS

WHEN spring fever, that disturbing malady, begins to run in our blood during late winter, we are apt to buy a railroad ticket or polish up the car and hasten southward to see the Azaleas bloom, or perhaps it will be the Cherry blossoms along the Potomac, or the Apple blossoms in the gracious valley of the Shenandoah. But have we not in our haste missed a potent easement of our unrest right at home—the blossoming of the Snowdrops? Theirs is a fragile but hardy celebration that takes place in the very teeth of winter and seems to me one of the most stirring and heartening demonstrations of the whole year. To see these tender organisms intrepidly forcing their way upward through the frozen earth and unfolding their snowy bells in the face of such elemental terrors as prevail in the northern winter is a sight curious enough to engage our attention and brave enough to stiffen our spines. Poets and ordinary persons alike recognize Lilac time, Rose time, even Iris time, but Snowdrop time goes unheralded and unsung.

I have always thought that the time when Snowdrops bloom should be given some preëminence, but the trouble is that seldom does anyone in this country plant enough Snowdrops to produce those sheets of living frost that thousands blossoming together bring about. A thousand Daffodils or Tulips make a grand show, a thousand Snowdrops are a mere handful in the vast emptiness of the winter landscape. But a thousand, or even five hundred, are a step towards later realization, for Snowdrops happily situated increase steadily and sturdily, and if we plant the different species we may quite easily span the bereft period from the time when winter's cold hand fairly clutches us until spring begins her first delicate approaches.

Not, of course, in localities where the snow lies deep the winter through and bitter cold is the rule for months on end will Snowdrops bloom out-of-doors all winter, but where the winter knows relenting moments now and again, when the sun shines warmly and the earth thaws a little under its genial glance, there certainly we may have them during January, February and March. I have occasionally had Snowdrops in December, but not often, and my garden is a cold one with a chill, clay soil as host and the climatic exigencies of New York State as nurse—or the other way round. And I have known Snowdrops to force their way upwards in midwinter through solid ice and blossom, each surrounded by a tiny melted circle in the ice as if the chill little blossoms emanated a slight warmth before which the frigid element must needs give way.

There is surprisingly little general knowledge about Snowdrops. Even more than was Peter Bell's Primrose nothing more to him than a yellow Primrose, so a Snowdrop to nine persons out of ten is a mere Snowdrop; what kind of Snowdrop is not known at all. As a matter of fact there are a number of species. The

Snowdrops

Kew Hand-List recognizes twelve species and a number of varieties, and there are more. The differences between them are perhaps not great; chiefly they consist in size of bell, width of leaf, height and, most important to the gardener, time of blossoming. There is also considerable variety of habitat resulting in diverse needs which must be taken into consideration if those sheets of frosted whiteness are to be attained that so brighten the dawn of the year. Let me here quote Sir William Lawrence, Bart., V.M.H., an authority upon the subject:

"Snowdrops may be roughly divided into two classes, namely, the Snowdrops of Northern and Southeastern Europe, and those that come from Greece, Russia, Turkey, and Asia Minor. The former, of which *Galanthus nivalis,* the common Snowdrop, is the type, will grow on a slope or on the level. They prefer a shady position, cool and moist without being damp, and whilst at rest do not seem to mind being grown over as long as the herbage dies down completely in winter. Of the other group, *G. Elwesii* and the Crimean Snowdrop, *G. plicatus,* seem to prefer a stony slope, well drained and dry in summer. In planting in such a position care must be taken that the stones do not interfere with the young shoots. In this group also come the Snowdrops which bloom before Christmas, such as *olgae, bizantinus* and *cilicicus.* These require all the sun they can get."

For many years I made the mistake of treating all Snowdrops alike to a shaded position and so came to the conclusion that *Elwesii, plicatus* and some of the others were short-lived and unreliable. This is not at all the case, but it may be said with some certainty that they do not require in our climate the same amount of sunshine that they do in the moister atmosphere of the British Isles. Sun for part of the day is sufficient.

Now before we come to discuss specific kinds, a few remarks of a general character may be in order. In the first place it is important to secure the bulbs of Snowdrops as early as possible, preferably in August, and to get them into the ground immediately. A nourishing but not rich soil is the best for the general run of them; in heavy, overfed soils they are habitually short-lived. A mixture of leaf mold and light loam with a little sand seems ideal for them. In this the bulbs should be planted from three to four inches deep from the top of the bulb, and about two inches apart for the small kinds and from three to four for the giants of the race. When planted they should be left alone. Their increase is principally from offsets, and, though they may be moved with safety at almost any season, our aim is to have them form fine thrifty clumps, which they can do only when left in peace and not harried by continual lifting. Most kinds seed freely when happily situated, but the seed commonly takes from a year onwards to germinate. Nevertheless our store of Snowdrops is appreciably increased in time by this means. The seed may be rubbed into the ground about the parent clump or sown in pans sunk in a cool place.

It is well known that Snowdrops are happiest when growing among the roots of other plants, and we may take advantage of this fact to bring about many a pleasant early picture in the garden. The neighborhood of such early-comers as the Asiatic Witch Hazels, Spice

Snowdrops

Bush, Pussy Willow, red-stemmed Dogwoods, *Cornus mas, Daphne Mezereum,* and *Daphne Blagayana* is becoming and congenial to them. They may also be grown among Christmas Roses, Lenten Roses, Hepaticas, Ferns, Winter Aconites, and such small bulbous things as the early Crocuses, Leucojums, and Scillas.

I cannot pretend to a knowledge of all the Snowdrops, but as the saying goes, I am on my way. Particularly are some of the earliest kinds still unknown to me. Mr. Bowles says, "Now that it is easy to have Snowdrops in our gardens from October to April it is worth our while to seek and grow those that will carry on the succession throughout that period. The Greek forms of *Galanthus nivalis, G. olgae* and *G. racheliae,* open the Snowdrop season, and by the time that the green markings of these then leafless forms are fading out *G. cilicicus,* with its sea-blue leaves well developed, should be showing buds."

None of these species grows in my garden, but then comes *byzantinus,* which in milder climates than mine will surely blossom in December. It is the first to bloom with me, never failing to appear in January. This grand Snowdrop is supposed to be a natural hybrid between *Elwesii* and *plicatus* and comes from about Constantinople. It has the conspicuous plicate foliage of the latter, the large globular flowers carried on tall stems and richly marked with green on the inner tube. Some think it the finest of all Snowdrops. A friend in Ohio writes me that it always blooms in his garden before Christmas, growing in light woodland. Snowdrops do not as a rule force well, but if one is going to attempt this operation *byzantinus* is the species to use.

[13]

What Happens in My Garden

When the blossoms of *byzantinus* are at their best appears *Elwesii*, bold and assured in the face of winter storm and stress. In sheltered situations it seldom fails to bloom before January has run its course. It comes from Asia Minor, from an altitude of from three to four thousand feet, and is one of the kinds too often given a shaded, dampish situation when what it ardently desires is a stony slope, sun and drought in summer. It is a splendid species; blossoms large, oblong-roundish in shape, the leaves stout and channeled and somewhat glaucous. In propitious seasons I have known blossoms on my patch from early in January until the beginning of April. There are several forms of *G. Elwesii*, but the only one I see listed this year is *Whittallii*, said to be the giant of this branch of the family. It is on my autumn list, for claims are made that it is taller and altogether more robust than *Elwesii*.

Another early-blooming species, which, however, seems to have some late-blooming forms, is *G. plicatus*, known as the Great Crimean Snowdrop. It has a largish bulb, neatly brown-coated, which sends up two glaucous leaves sometimes to a height of a foot or more and noticeably broad, their edges curiously folded back, by which peculiarity this species may be distinguished from others of the clan. *G. plicatus* is found in southern Russia near the shores of the Baltic and is quite hardy; indeed it is one of the easiest and most reliable kinds to grow, increasing satisfactorily on any loamy slope with shade for part of the day only.

But if I could have but one Snowdrop I am sure it would be the little common kind I have known all my life, *Galanthus nivalis*. In certain localities in this country, though Gray does not mention it, it has gone native and sheets occasional hillsides with its peculiar frosty whiteness in February and March. I remember such a hillside in Maryland where I played as a little girl that was literally alive with Snowdrops in winter, as it was later shimmering with Dogtooth Violets.

G. nivalis is neither so early-flowering nor so showy as the larger-flowered kinds but it is a lovely thing, a grand doer, a most gratifying spreader, and its virginal scent is a delight. It loves a lightly wooded hillside, a place where Ferns and Bloodroot and Dutchman's Breeches thrive, and I know of no sight more heartening on a winter day than its fountains of frosty bells and arching slender leaves. If I possessed a wood it should harbor thousands; if only a shaded shrubbery it should be carpeted with them; if only the north side of a rock garden I would tuck in as many as possible. These little storm troops of the year are a most precious possession, and unless you spend your winters in the city you will want plenty of them.

I like the common single form best, but the double sort is quaintly opulent and engaging. It is said that single Snowdrops have a tendency to go double, but this has not proved true in my experience; rather the reverse has happened—the doubles go single. There are other forms of *nivalis*, among them *maximus; viridi-apice*, with greener tips; *imperati*, a fine Italian form with charming widespread blossoms, but perhaps a doubtful constitution; and *procularis*, lacking the usual green stain; but these are difficult to come by, and the little common kind and its double form will satisfy most of us.

What Happens in My Garden

On my list to secure this early autumn if possible are various other Snowdrop species, chief among them *G. icariae,* a form of *latifolius* from the island of Nikaria off the coast of Asia Minor. It is said to be a beauty with emerald-stained blossoms exceeding an inch in length, the plant growing a foot high. If it is secured it must be given a warm position under a south wall or against a south-facing rock in the rock garden. *G. Fosteri,* also from Asia Minor, is likewise on my list. It has been called the King of Snowdrops, and its foliage is broad and blunt; but it is scarce, and doubtless I shall not find it. If you read Mr. Bowles' "My Garden in Spring" your Snowdrop wants will sprout and flourish, and you will probably sigh in vain for many of them. But sighing for the unobtainable is as much a part of gardening as rejoicing over the obtained—or weeding. It is all part of the game. But plant a thousand Snowdrops this autumn and so take the sting from winter's frosts.

CHAPTER III

THE Tulips known as "Early" do not by any means receive the recognition that their special comeliness and usefulness merit. So many, so marvelous, so acclaimed are the Darwins, Breeders, and the Cottage varieties of the later season that too often the early-flowering kinds are quite overlooked in our plans for spring's adornment. They suffer too, these early varieties, by association in our minds with pots and geometrical bedding, for which they are indeed ideally adapted. But these are not the only rôles they are capable of filling with grace and distinction. Once a bedding plant always a bedding plant is the dictum under which they too often unjustly suffer. But there is a pleasant surprise awaiting those who cast precedent aside and allow this type of Tulip to play a more gracious and less formal part in the spring scene.

The Early Tulips are commonly large of flower and shortish and stoutish of stem. They come into bloom at the height of the Daffodil season, thus prolonging our Tulip enjoyment by at least two weeks, for the period between the earliest of the "Earlies" and the first May-flowering kinds is bridged by a number of varieties of what might be termed intermediates, of which Couleur Cardinal is a well known example. The color

[17]

of these Tulips is usually frank and clear, the texture of the petals somewhat thin, so that they have an almost transparent quality, a shining look, and many of them have a fine sweet scent. Then too, they are commonly less expensive than the later flowering kinds, and this is a consideration to be heeded in these days when our aim is to keep our gardens as gay and cheerful as possible with the minimum of expense.

I have found too, that several years of good service may be had of these early Tulips without lifting and with only a slight diminution of size, if the soil in which they are planted has not been too heavily and freshly manured. This slight falling off in size indeed seems to me no drawback, for just as I like Hyacinths best when a few years of border life have reduced their obese opulence, so I like Tulips (this is rank heresy, I know) when they have lost something of their self-conscious hugeness and take their places a bit more simply in the garden scene. Of course when they are used for bedding they must all be of a like size, and I dare say the larger the better, but when they are scattered about the beds and borders in clumps as we plant Daffodils, we can afford to subscribe to a less conventional standard. Thus planted, they add immensely to the gaiety of the early garden, especially if combined with certain herbaceous plants of their season or placed near some of the lovely early-flowering shrubs and trees, of which there are many.

And how many and enchanting are the varieties to be had, old and new, double and single! The double flowering kinds are to me especially delightful; they have a prim Victorian air that is most engaging, and they are splendid for cutting. A new one to me this year was Mystery of India, a beautiful flower on a sturdy eleven-inch stem, the petals dyed in soft tones of apricot and bronze with pinkish high lights. No words of mine can describe how lovely it was, growing near a bush of that finest shrub of recent introduction *Viburnum Carlesii*. A superb variety of more recent introduction and quite different coloring is Orange Nassau. It is said to be one of the many sports of Murillo but bears no resemblance to it, save perhaps in shape. The color is the most stirring orange-red with brownish lights, and the stem is sturdy and upright. It is still somewhat dear in price but well worth making a sacrifice for if you feel the need of a glorious blob of color somewhere about your domain. For cutting it is unsurpassed. Vuurbaak is a less expensive Tulip of bright orange-scarlet coloring among the double-flowered earlies.

Among the pink doubles delightful choice may be made. Extremely inexpensive and perennially charming is the old Murillo, mother of many sports, so to speak, and garbed in a most lovely pale pink and white ensemble. Little more expensive is one of these sports, Peachblossom by name, very double, very gay, with bright pink flowers flushed white. It is especially lovely for cutting. Triumphator is a newer variety and very lovely among pink Tulips, and the still more recent Azalea when combined with the fleecy blossoms of the little Pie Cherry, either in a broad-mouthed jar or in the garden, is one of the best, a soft pink flower flushed with deeper color. So much for the pink kinds.

The yellows are also many and alluring. One of the

finest I have grown is the new Golden Giant, an immense semi-double flower, coming very early and lasting long, the color pure unblemished yellow and the flowers possessed of a fine fragrance. The beautiful amber-colored Maréchal Niel that combines so delightfully with Bleedingheart is magnificent, and in spite of the fact that one must dig deeply into the toe of the stocking to find its rather costly price, is almost a must-have. But there are cheaper kinds: Mr. Van der Hoef is fine, very full and gleaming with a satin sheen, and there is the old Yellow Rose, weak of stem, heavy-headed, but of a color to light the eyes and a scent that enchants the nose. It is so inexpensive as to be had almost for the proverbial song. It flowers later than the general run of the "earlies." Tea Rose (Safrano, Brimstone) is another extremely inexpensive and lovely old variety that foams along the edges of borders amid *Anchusa myosotidiflora,* purple Violas and pink Flowering Almonds with the most enchanting effect. Its color is primrose-yellow with the same flushing of apricot that is found in its namesake the Safrano Rose. Forget-me-nots are the perfect accompaniment for these yellow Tulips.

The prestige of Schoonoord, the snow-white Murillo sport, as the best white double early Tulip, has never been questioned. It is an old variety but invaluable. Boule de Neige is also desirable, very full and double like a white Peony.

Before speaking of the single early Tulips I want to describe a delightful planting of double early Tulips I saw last spring at the International Garden Club on the old Pell estate, Bartow, on Pelham Bay. About a square pool in the sunken garden directly behind the gracious old manor house is a simple but formal arrangement of beds. These were planted in pink double Tulips of two tones, those in the inside beds very pale, those in the outer ones deeper. In the flagged paths that bisect the garden, pale citron Alyssum grew luxuriantly, introducing a charming color note. Used as accents in the four corners of the garden, great bushes of the Star Magnolia, *M. stellata,* were in full bloom, and in the border against the enclosing walls were bushes of pink Flowering Almond, lavender Hyacinths and masses of purple Pansies. Across this expanse of lovely color one looked at the blue waters of Long Island Sound. A more gracious and enchanting spring scene could hardly be imagined.

It is difficult to know where to begin with single early Tulips, so many are my favorites. I like especially those of pink or pink-and-white coloring and have enjoyed several that were new to me this past spring. One was Alice Roosevelt, wearing a charming soft tone of pink and very fragrant. It made a nice spot of color among purple Violas. Another was Diadem, still expensive but of the most lovely bland color tone. A small group of it beneath a dwarf apple tree with Grape Hyacinths and white Narcissi was most attractive. The old Proserpine, an enormous round carmine-pink flower, is good and delightfully fragrant, and both Rose Luisante and Flamingo (not to be confused with the May-flowering variety of that name) are excellent, the former rose-pink and of good substance, the latter a full pure pink with a white rib down the center of each delicately crinkled petal. It makes a charming picture with mats of the Heliotrope-scented, double-flowered Arabis. And I am not sure that for bedding the dainty pink and white Cottage Maid, though now missing from many catalogues, as is that rare enchantress Jenny, has ever been equaled.

A Tulip of rather unusual coloring and fine rounded shape is Lady Moore. The color of this kind is soft reddish copper, and the flower has a delicate fragrance.

One of the finest of all early Tulips is De Wet. Its extraordinarily luminous effect is produced by a network of scarlet veins laid upon a warm orange ground. No other Tulip has just this effect, though the Mayflowering Argo when mature approaches it and is a fine thing. Nor must the fine fragrance of De Wet be forgotten; it is not the least of its attractions. I like this glowing flower massed against evergreens with rich purple Pansies or Violas as a foreground. If we are in a saving mood Fred Moore may be used in its place, and a gay picture for little cost be staged with Forsythia, Poetaz Narcissus, and mats of *Phlox subulata* G. F. Wilson. I have such a planting in my garden that has been in place for six years, and it seems to me the Tulips are lovelier every year. Fred Moore is a very fragrant Tulip.

Of yellow early Tulips there are many good kinds. Rising Sun is one with especially large flowers of deep golden yellow color. I like to plant patches of it near the spread of white-flowered Dogwood trees. Yellow Queen is an excellent variety somewhat taller than earlies generally, as indeed is Rising Sun. Yellow Queen is paler in color though deepening at the edges. For bedding Mon Tresor and Goldfinch are unsurpassed, the former being particularly fine in form. The lighter yellow Early Tulips make particularly attractive and springlike beds over floors of pale English Daisies. And I have seen charming effects where standard Wistarias rose from beds of yellow Tulips carpeted with purple Pansies. Standard Wistarias might also be used above beds of pink Tulips carpeted with Arabis. In my old garden in Rockland County four standard Wistarias punctuated the width of the garden, and in the beds at their feet flowed a stream of scarlet and white early Tulips. The effect was enchantingly gay. The Tulips used were White Swan, one of the most graceful of its kind, and the sweet-scented and brilliant *T. gesneriana spathulata major*, which is not a true early but flowers with White Swan.

There are numerous other desirable early-flowering Tulips—Van der Neer, a fine purple kind; the old scarlet Prince of Austria, with its delicious scent, rather detracting yellow base, and long lasting qualities; Cullinan, a pale primrose flower with a delicate rose edge, and the always popular Le Rêve, or Hobbeme, with its strangely lovely blending of rose and fawn and a finely rounded form. But enough has been said, I think, to show that the early Tulips have a charm of their own and a very definite usefulness.

Some shrubs and plants that bloom with them and with which they may be combined are the following: Wistaria, Japanese Quince, Flowering Almond, Double-Flowering Peach, *Spiraea Thunbergii, Prunus tomentosa*, Cherry, *Magnolia stellata, Syringa oblata*, Dogwood, pink and white, Forsythia, Arabis, double and single, pink or white, *Anchusa myosotidiflora*, Merten-

sia, *Pulmonaria angustifolia* (these three are blue),
Bleedingheart, Pansies, Violas, English Daisies, *Phlox
subulata* G. F. Wilson, or the white *Nelsoni*, Grape
Hyacinth, Daffodils, Poet's Narcissi, Primroses, Cow-
slips, and many more.

CHAPTER IV

THE CELANDINE, A FLOWER OF THE POETS

ALL who were brought up on the soothing pap of the Victorian poets are familiar with the name of Celandine. It makes a song in the mind as do Violet, Kingcup, and Cowslip. Many a poet of that period made use of this small flower, which makes its punctual appearance while wintry winds still rage and "we've little warmth or none," to point a moral or adorn a tale. But it was in particular Wordsworth's flower as were the most famous stanzas written in celebration of its "kindly, unassuming spirit." So greatly did he admire the brightly varnished stars gleaming against their mat of shining green, and so closely are they associated with his name, that their likeness is carved upon his tomb.

The Celandine—the Lesser Celandine, as it is usually called—was the flower of poets and children and simple country folk who, as a matter of fact, often have the same loves. Reading old books, one learns that such as these have long warmed their spirits at its cheery matutinal flickering, and found various remedial uses for its little tuberous roots. This is amply testified to by the various names it has acquired as it crept down the centuries, sure sign of the tender regard in which it was held by the country folk. Smallwort, it has been called, and Pilewort, Figwort, because of the shape of its clusters of little figlike tubers, and for obvious reasons Bright Eyes, Gilty Cup, Goldy Knob, Brights, Golden Guineas, and so on. *Ranunculus ficaria* is its botanical name, but I am sure it is seldom used—too grand a name for such a simple flower. Wordsworth well described its character and habits when he wrote:

> *Careless of thy neighbourhood,*
> *Thou dost show thy pleasant face*
> *On the moor, and in the wood,*
> *In the lane;—there's not a place,*
> *Howsoever mean it be,*
> *But 'tis good enough for thee.*

But there are nearly always two sides to an opinion, and while poets and children and simple folk have long loved the Celandine, in England and in Europe where it is native, thoroughgoing gardeners, it seems, have not. It is more often than not harshly spoken of by these as a tiresome and graceless weed. Linnaeus, who knelt upon the sod before the glory of the Gorse, is one who apparently had no eye for the sheen of this lowly plant, for he strongly recommends to farmers its summary extirpation from pasture lands because of the space taken by the little tubers and because fastidious cattle will not eat it. And Mr. Bowles in our own day, so generally gentle toward plant life, says in "My Garden in Spring," "With the common wild forms one constantly struggles but cannot entirely expel from the garden."

Of course if one is the kind of person who counts the spoons night and morning and can name to a head the Tulips, Irises, and Phloxes that grow in one's garden, barring burglars and more than commonly en-

The Celandine, a Flower of the Poets

terprising weeds, life will hold few surprises. But I was
surprised when Wordsworth's Celandine appeared in
my garden, though I did not then, nor for several years
afterwards, know it for what it was. It was on an
April morning some eight years ago that I first came
upon it, a little spread of dark, heart-shaped leaves all
decked out in highly varnished yellow stars on a
roughish piece of grow-as-you-please bank that skirts
the east side of my acre. It was one of those surprises,
perhaps undeserved, that come to those who do not
too anxiously order their gardens. I was enchanted
with it. Later, when I came to know its true identity,
I learned from Gray's "New Manual of Botany" that
the Lesser Celandine is found occasionally in damp
places from Massachusetts to the District of Columbia,
introduced from Eurasia. It seems likely that it came
with the early settlers from the old country, its unconsidered figlets entangled among the more precious roots
of some prized plant, and that it has been prowling about
in fence corners and along roadsides ever since, a little
weedling ghost, seeking a place to rest, or perhaps a
poet to appreciate its glinty charms.

It has not proved a weed or in any way an incon-
venience since it appeared uninvited in my garden. It
is far from "studding the meadows and hedge-banks
and carpeting thin woodland" (had I these spacious
adjuncts) as it is reported to do in England. But its
mat of glossy, brittle heart-shaped leaves has gradually
widened to perhaps the size of a large meat platter and
one or two subsidiary colonies have started farther
along the bank. I should be distressed if spring came
and it did not. It blossoms with *Scilla sibirica*, that

[27]

also occupies the bank, the two forgathering with enthusiasm and making the most brilliant color contrast in the garden of any season—piercing blue and brightest yellow. A small show close to the ground, but none is more striking; and to its credit it is willingly produced in the shade where it is often difficult to fix bright colors.

The blossoms of the Lesser Celandine open only in shining weather. The little green knobs unfold about nine in the morning, and by five in the afternoon have closed for the night. Then as the days grow longer and warmer the whole plant disappears, leaves, flowers and stems. I have never noted just the date of its final disappearance, but it is accomplished quickly and quietly. There simply comes a day when it is not there.

Mr. Bowles, after talking about expulsion, speaks with enthusiasm of a white form of the Lesser Celandine as a fine thing "that has a charming, creamy tint and is as beautifully varnished as any Buttercup." He also tells us of a double form that he considers worth growing, and of one he found with variegated leaves. None of these forms have I ever been able to come upon in this country though I have inquired assiduously, and should like well to have the white one. But he also speaks of "the major form from Italy," which he says does not increase too quickly, and this I have had for many years. It came to me as did so many treasured things from the garden of the late Clarence Lown in Poughkeepsie.

This type grows perhaps six inches tall and to the eyes of the casual has the general appearance of our Marsh Marigold, *Caltha palustris*. The leaves are large, shining and handsome, the flowers like giant Buttercups with that effective highly varnished surface. The plants bloom almost as early as the more humble sort and as inconspicuously take themselves off when they have finished. It seems to be variously known as *Ficaria grandiflora, Ficaria calthaefolia* and *Ranunculus grandiflora*. But by any name it is a valuable plant and makes a brave show in the early spring garden. It grows here in a low portion of the rock garden where the soil is dark and seldom bone-dry. Near it are clumps of Spring Snowflakes, *Leucojum vernum,* and a little higher up out of the damp gatherings of soft-hued early Crocuses—*Imperati, Sieberi, Tomasinianus.* The spread of this Celandine is slow unless in stirring the ground about it you disengage from the parent clump some of the little tubers. Any of these will start off on their own to make new clumps, and so your store and your pleasure increase.

Curiously enough the plant we know as the Greater Celandine has no relationship or likeness to the Lesser Celandine or its *grandiflora* type. It does not belong as do these to the natural order Ranunculaceae, but to the Poppy tribe. Its botanical name is *Chelidonium majus,* and it is commonly known by any of a number of appellations, including Wartwort, Tetterwort, Killwort, Kinningwort, Sightwort, Swallowwort, Garden Celandine, and Greater Celandine. It is as well known in this country as in its native haunts in Europe, for it is one of the plants that have faithfully followed the footsteps of man, or that man has carried with him in his wanderings. It was esteemed a famous remedy for a vast number of ills that flesh and pride are heirs to—"baldness, blackspots, chaps, chollicke, dropsie, jaundice and scurvy, ringworm, green-sores, freckles, teethache, falling teeth, itch, plague, bloodshot eyes, hot gout, fellons"—to name but a few of the long list given in that curious ancient work, "The Garden of Health," by Langham, 1579. Small wonder we find it lurking about old farmsteads and along the roads near long-settled towns rather than in more secluded localities. Such a valuable remedy for "Sicknesse generall" and "Griefes generall" must certainly have been kept close at hand by our adventuring ancestors, who on coming to the New World faced so many dangers to life and limb and spirit.

This plant, according to Mrs. Grieve in "A Modern Herbal," is undoubtedly the true Celandine, the famous drug plant of the Middle Ages, though the early herbalists seem to have used the name rather indiscriminately, confusing these two quite different-appearing plants, the Lesser and the Greater Celandine, in their writings.

Chelidonium majus is a herbaceous perennial growing some two feet tall, much branched, with hairy stems and flimsy though rather hairy leaves that are deeply divided and of a pale green, paler beneath. The flowers, borne in a loose cluster at the ends of the stems, consist of four ocher-colored petals set in the form of a cross, with a dense mass of yellow stamens in the center. Any frequenter of the countryside must know the plant, especially if he has attempted to gather the cheerful blossoms and so has had his fingers badly stained with the ill-smelling yellow juice with which the stems are stored, and which country people still maintain is a cure for warts. But it is no good for cutting in any case, for leaves and flowers wilt almost immediately. It is pretty, however, and especially noticeable in early spring, and the plants bloom all summer, often bearing their yellow crossed flowers and their long seed-pods at the same time, which gives the plant a rather untidy appearance.

Pliny, whose book of wonders was called by D'Israeli an "awful repository of all the errors of antiquity," records the discovery of this plant by the swallows, affirming that it is named Chelidon (a swallow) because it comes into flower when the swallows arrive and its departure coincides with theirs, and that these wise birds make use of its juices to cure eye affections of their young. Many curious notions were held about the plant in early times, and the belief in its effectiveness as a cure for eye troubles was held for a long time.

Of course, the Greater Celandine is a weed, and perhaps the careful gardener would not admit it to his garden; yet it covers a bare bank with pretty pale verdure and yellow flowers throughout spring and summer, so is not by any means to be despised. In the catalogue of one of the best known British plantsmen is listed *Chelidonium laciniatum*, "an odd and quaint variety of the Greater Celandine with handsome leaves and pretty fringed flowers." And seed is offered of a double-flowered sort that is said to be quite well worth growing.

A plant whose leaves and flowers are much like those of the Greater Celandine is native in this country. This is the Celandine Poppy, *Stylophorum diphyllum*, found at the edges of dampish woodlands in many parts of the East and out through the central western states.

This plant is sometimes transplanted from the wild to gardens, and I have occasionally seen it offered in catalogues as a good rock plant. The flowers are somewhat smaller than those of the Chelidonium, but they appear early; and the stems exude the same orange-colored juice.

Perhaps none of these plants that bear the name of Celandine will meet the fancy of the exquisite gardener. Certainly they are not to be numbered among choice and difficult things; but they are cheerful and willing and bright in appearance, and one's experience with them will not be like that of the husband in A. A. Milne's story "Two People," who "watched a sow-thistle which had got into his sidalceas change into a sidalcea that had got into his sow-thistles." They will not ring such disconcerting changes upon us, but prove equal to maintaining their individuality even in the face of invading thistles.

CHAPTER V

AGAINST a background of moist earth, dark tree trunks, twisted brier, and straightened shrub, with last year's leaves clinging here and there, the fabric of Spring's garment is wonderfully woven, pale yellowish green and greenish yellow, swept here and there with white, seemingly dropped from Winter's bag of tricks as he scurries away toward the north. It is delicately patterned in Adonis and Daffodil, Spicebush and Forsythia and Shadblow, Snowdrop and Snowflake, Winter Aconite and Anemone, Christmas Rose and Dandelion, white Violet and Troutlily.

This yellow and white color scheme is a pleasing one, young and infinitely fresh. It arouses the imagination and releases winter-bound senses. But the eye is greedy. It asks a fillip. Something to touch this tentative beauty to pulsating life, to compliment it and incite it to gaiety. And what is there to bring about this desirable metamorphosis? Why, that magic hue we call blue, to be sure—true blue, not vague lilacs or sad purples, but bright, pure blue. We have but to look about us and note how the blue sky above brings out all the latent delicacy as well as the strength of the frail vernal harmony to know how much this celestial hue will do for us at garden level.

[33]

Blue is a lovely and beloved color at any season in the garden, but in the spring it is, verily, the salt in the broth.

Now let us see what is at hand. Happily the spring is wealthy in blue flowers, though they are largely exotic and do not spring from our own soil—for Violets can by no stretch of the imagination be called blue. The gardener, however, is not held down by native lack in this matter but reaches out to the four corners of the earth and gathers what he has need of—or at least as much as our crippling quarantine laws will permit him to grasp. In our own spacious wild we have the Hepatica, blue enough at times, though more often white or pale purple, the little Quaker Lady (Houstonia) that sweeps the spring meadows with pale blue frost, the Virginia Cowslip (Mertensia), and out in the West a number of Polemoniums, the little known Synthyrises, the bulbous plant *Brodiaea laxa*.

But from foreign parts we derive, and should make lavish use of, a number of little blue-flowered bulbs. These increase with kindly alacrity if their needs be ever so slightly considered. Their usefulness in the spring garden cannot be oversung.

Earliest to appear in my garden, even before the fiercely burning blue torches of the Siberian Squill, are the cheeky little pencil points of *Hyacinthus azureus* (*Muscari azureum*) that rise only a few inches high between strap-shaped leaves in early March—sometimes, indeed, in February. They are paler blue than the Scilla, and you will notice that the lower flowers on the little cone open first, and that they open wide like bells and not in the intermediate manner common to the house of Muscari. This delightful small spring flower, just right for a foreground planting of Snow-flakes (Leucojums), seems not to be much used here-abouts. Nor is its later flowering sister, *Hyacinthus amethystinus,* called the Alpine Hyacinth, that comes from the Pyrenees and heights in Croatia. This kind hangs out rather large bells along a slender stalk that may be eight or ten inches tall. These bells are blue but have a hint of veiled purple, and the bulbs are sometimes found in catalogues listed as *Muscari ame-thystinum.* Both will flourish anywhere out of the way of the intolerant hoe and are especially good company along a half-woodsy path where the soil is good and nourishing.

Happily every one plants *Scilla sibirica*—surely the bluest thing in all nature. There are few gardens wherein it does not follow hard upon the heels of the Snowdrops and Winter Aconites, often catching them up and conspiring with them to make a brilliant small show. The blue of *Scilla bifolia* is less curt than that of *S. sibirica,* but it comes earlier and sometimes, says the late W. R. Dykes, "among collected bulbs specimens appear with crimson anthers, to which the varietal name of *taurica* has been given." Both these are well worth including, chiefly for their earliness. Scillas increase rapidly, and any one may have sheets of bright blue color in the spring garden who will let them have free rein in any half-shaded situation where the soil is rich in humus.

The later flowering Scillas, or Spanish and English Bluebells, *S. campanulata* and *S. festalis* (*S. nutans*) come in a rather poorish pink, as well as the blues and a fine frosted white. The blue-flowered kinds are the best, however, though not nearly so strong in color as the earlier forms. *S. campanulata* is stiffer and more upright than the English Bluebell (*festalis*), and the different kinds make fine interplantings for Darwin and Cottage Tulips with which they bloom. *S. festalis* hangs its bells from a little crook, and it is these that one sees making pools of dim color in shadowy spring woodlands in England. They increase rapidly and need to be divided every few years.

Chionodoxas (Glories of the Snow), that to the non-botanical eye appear much like Scillas, are members of a small genus native in Crete and Asia Minor. *C. sardensis,* that gets its name from the ancient town of Sardis near which it grows at stark and high elevations, wears as bright and hard a blue as *Gentiana acaulis. C. Luciliae* is modified by a white central zone, and the body color varies from pale to deep sky-blue. These are the more lovely, and strewn thickly about a planting of that gay early Tulip, *T. Kaufmanniana,* or spread with a lavish hand beneath the creamy-flowered *Magnolia stellata,* make a very brave early picture to feast the eyes upon. Those who have a weakness for size may plant *C. gigantea* (*C. grandiflora* or *Allenii*), which is bigger but no better, and the color sometimes runs to mauve. Or one may plant *C. Tmolusi,* unpronounceable but serving to prolong the season, and a fine thing though the color that rings the white zone leans to purple—but does not achieve it. This kind is a plant of rich valleys where the soil is kept moist during the growing season by melting snows from above; do not give it too dry a place in the garden.

True Blues Among the Early Blossoms

The Muscaris are the friendliest of bulbous things, increasing by offsets and by seeds with prodigal generosity. The Common Grape Hyacinth, *M. botryoides,* has naturalized itself in certain neighborhoods, and a delightful surprise it is to find this pretty alien holding its own in the rough grass of meadow and roadside. Do not admit the Muscaris to your rock garden (they are too "spreadacious," as a friend says), but give them the freedom of your banks and braes and shrubbery borders. Heavenly Blue, a supposed form of *M. conicum,* like good wine, surely needs no bush. Its bright blue cones scent the garden with the delicious aroma of Clove Pink in April. I like these everywhere—wadded between the crimson shoots of Peonies, shooting up through mats of Arabis, Aubrietia, or Creeping Phlox, spread to make a blue floor for Cherry blossoms to fall upon.

There are others of this clan, too, that may be touched here only in passing, but that are worth growing: *Argaei,* dwarf, very dark blue bells with white tips; *armenicum,* late, deep blue and spicy; *micranthum,* bright narrow cones; *neglectum,* the so-called Black Muscari; *paradoxum,* dark also and shaped somewhat like a sugar loaf, and *racemosum,* said to be sweet-scented, which I have never seen. By the way, the Muscaris await a careful monographer; the genus is in confusion. None is difficult to grow, seemingly, and most are desirable. The little few-belled *M. Heldreichi* I have never been able to secure for my garden.

So much for bulbs. Then of course there are the blue-flowered Anemones, for which exquisite innocents, because of our quarantine against plant introduction, we must pay a king's ransom, if we can get them at all. Whereas in less anxiously "protected" countries the lovely blue Apennine Anemone may be had for as low as twopence each, the peerless *A. blanda* for little more. And so on. What a price we pay for our so-called blessings! A few pre-quarantine colonies in my rock garden make me ache each spring that I may not have them as they are enjoyed abroad, starring the woodland and the rock garden with their winsome beauty. I feel very much like the little boy of my acquaintance who said he would like his mother all right if she did not have such an awful lot to say about everything he wanted to do.

Well, if we may not have the precious blue Anemones, there is still the old blue Lungwort, *Pulmonaria angustifolia,* to fall back upon, though it has grown scarce of late in catalogues. Why, I don't know. It is a vigorous low tufted plant with long roughish leaves above which, about Daffodil time, appear in conspicuous profusion pink buds that open to purest blue. It will thrive even under trees, and indeed grow best in partial shade. I use it with *Anchusa myosotidiflora,* Heavenly Blue Grape Hyacinths, and Forget-me-nots to maintain a succession of bright blue on the edges of my rock garden.

Anchusa myosotidiflora, like a giant dark blue Forget-me-not and blooming before it, is invaluable. It grows well in shade or sun, but likes a soil that is not too dry. It has a thousand uses in the garden. It wreathes the yellow skirts of the Forsythias with lovely effect, is lovely in low borders with early Trollius, Doronicum, and blue and white Camassias, is lovely as as an interplanting for Tulips of almost any color. Try it with some of the "difficult" bronzes, as well as with those of purer hue. I have an old planting here of the Anchusa with the very inexpensive flame-colored Tulip Fred Moore that always brings many complimentary remarks from visitors to the garden. The Anchusa enjoys a long season. It is, I believe, now properly known as *Brunnera macrophylla.*

Polemoniums also twang away at a song of spring "blues," albeit a tender one. The old Jacob's Ladder, *Polemonium caeruleum,* blooms in May. Earlier is the little *P. reptans,* close to the ground and pretty for the rock garden. I forgot it when mentioning our native blue spring flowers. It is good for a border, too, if not too closely pressed upon by stronger growing plants. From the Northwest we get *Polemonium pulcherrimum,* that travels under more than one alias, but Dr. Ira Gabrielson abides by *pulcherrimum,* which name indeed is suitable, for I believe it means "prettiest." It has grown in my garden for many years and self-sows freely, thus conveying to me the fact that all is well with it. Though a high mountain plant it accepts life in lowland gardens with surprising complacence. Its China-blue blossoms have bright orange-yellow eyes to set them off, and the leaves are more finely divided than those of *P. reptans.* Otherwise it is similar, though more showy altogether.

Mertensia virginica with its pallid leaves and azure nodding blossoms, often touched with pink, grows here in an effective association. In a low border where the soil is deep and rich a pink-flowered Crabapple, *Malus floribunda,* spreads widely its wreathed, crooked branches. Beneath it are clumps of Mertensia, grown

[39]

stout with the years, interplanted with crowding Poet's Narcissi. And if you are a "curious gardener" you will want to look up some of the western Mertensias. I can speak well especially of the Prairie Bluebell, *Mertensia lanceolata,* good for dryish places; of *M. ciliata,* the Mountain Bluebell, luxuriant and graceful with glaucous foliage and sprays of nodding pale blue flowers; of *M. pratensis,* described by Mr. Andrews as "a rare plant from the Spanish Peaks." In his fine book, "Western American Alpines," Dr. Gabrielson says: "The first sight of a Mertensia-covered hillside is simply breath-taking in loveliness, and there are areas in the Blue Mountains and northern Cascades where the Mertensia display is the equal of any spectacle in the West." He names several kinds unknown to me but procurable.

And then of course there are Forget-me-nots. These play an important part in every spring garden, whether they are used as a floor for Tulips in formal beds or to bind the edges of shrubberies and herbaceous borders, allowed to stream along woodland paths or to shimmer about the rock garden. There are many kinds. Earliest to bloom here is *Myosotis dissitiflora.* This kind is very gay and spready, sowing itself freely, almost too freely, about the rock garden and shrubbery borders. *M. sylvatica* is the kind to use along woodland paths and in the wild garden. It has a glorified form called Victoria and a fine white form known as White Lady. There is also a quite enchanting pink-flowered *sylvatica,* like the belongings of some dainty baby. *M. palustris grandiflora* and *M. p. semperflorens* are for damp places, and the latter blooms practically all the season. *M.*

rupicola is a choice species for the rock garden, a four-inch bit of gaiety with a bright yellow eye in its bright blue flower. There are many fine forms of *M. alpestris,* used commonly for bedding, among them Star of Love (very early), large-flowered and compact; Triumph, also early; Ruth Fisher, an old favorite; Blue Beauty, that is said (by its sponsors) to have a "columnlike growth covered from the foot upwards with large handsome deep blue flowers." Surely a prize!

There are many small blue-flowered plants that help to make a sparkle in the spring rock garden. Briefly here are a few: *Gentiana verna* and *G. acaulis, Aquilegia caerulea,* Globularias of sorts, dim and fuzzy and pretty; *Ajuga reptans,* the kind with metallic leaves that is so nice near the early-flowering Geums; *Linum perenne* and *L. alpinum; Omphalodes verna* and *O. cappadocica* (captious with me), *Sisyrinchium bermudianum, Lithospermum prostratum, Brodiaea capitata* and *B. congesta;* the lovely blue Primroses and Polyanthus.

How could I forget Periwinkle! Periwinkle that opens a brave blue eye upon the very dawn of the year and often gives an azure wink just outside the gate of winter. I would no more have a garden without a lot of Periwinkle than I would without a lot of Daffodils. If you have a woodland path or a half-shaded border, line it thickly with the little white early Violet, *Viola blanda;* behind these wind a ribbon of Periwinkle, kept clipped to keep it in bounds; and behind these still make a riot of pale star Daffodils. What matter the stock market with a spring so wealthily caparisoned?

CHAPTER VI

LITTLE IRISES

EVER since I graduated as a gardener from just Zinnias and Marigolds, the Iris tribe has had a strong hold upon my affections. At first it was the old purple Iris found in a deserted dooryard and transplanted with loving and unnecessary care to my little spick-and-span new garden; then followed *florentina,* of the French gray ensemble, and from this onwards by swift and inevitable stages to the vast and ever increasing wealth of the bearded species, once known as German. These, however, in the course of no great time became an astonishing embarrassment. A root of some new kind prayerfully saved up for and obtained finally for a kinglet's ransom became almost overnight, seemingly, a drug on even the friendliest market. It spread like Duckweed, all widely advertised Iris diseases to the contrary notwithstanding. What you had paid so dearly for could not now be given away. I began to feel the same dull resentment towards these lovely flowers that I had towards our well-meaning but too vulnerable cat, Mr. S. (named in entire good faith for its donor). In season and out, there was always a plethora of kittens that it was necessary and at the same time impossible to get rid of by fair means. Various painful and foul means ensued. Finally Mr. S. himself, or herself— But we need not continue the unhappy story.

Little Irises

But so it fell out with the beautiful bearded Iris ladies. Having but a small place, I watched them quietly taking possession of the whole of it. I gave with lavish generosity to all and sundry until even the village refused to find homes for more of them. Then I threw the excess rainbow loveliness over the fence into the lane where they lay all winter, roots in air, and bloomed on time, their velvet cheeks in the dust, and seemingly in no wise chagrined. No pride at all, thought I. No self-respecting plant would behave in such a way. I lost most of my interest then and there in making a collection of the tall bearded ladies, yet could not exorcise the memory of their beauty. For the form and texture of an Iris flower is one of the loveliest things in all nature.

The answer to the dilemma was finally found in the wild species, chiefly the dwarfs, but including a few taller slender sorts that had special personality and some restraint about increase.

Today my collection of tall bearded varieties is hopelessly out of date; anything I have could be bought for a quarter, yet they are still lovelier than any dreams that I can conjure. And they are ruthlessly kept in check. Every year they are thinned out, chopped back, or otherwise curbed, and the excess roots cast callously into the ash cans on village clean-up day. And we feel safer.

With the little species no such horrid expedients are called for. Many of them increase in a self-respecting way, but I find there is always some one who is glad of a bit of this one or that. Others keep one guessing nicely or tax our skill to just the right amount. When it comes to the Californians I am frank to say that when I succeed with them it is by the grace of God rather than through any skill or knowledge of my own. When we were young our old Irish nurse used to say of us, "With you children whatever 'tis 'tain't." That is just where I stand with the California Irises, though I think I am on my way to a better understanding, of which more later. Such Irises as the Oncocyclus and Junos, with one exception, I do not attempt. They require facilities that I do not possess, and to possess these beauties in this country is well-nigh impossible.

Having disposed of the tall bearded varieties, I still cling to the dwarf forms lovingly. Such spreads of lovely color they make along the edges of the borders or in the rock garden. Their flowers are large and showy, their habit neatly squat. *Iris pumila caerulea* is a beauty and not too plentiful these days. It grows only a few inches tall, has large flowers of a soft atmospheric blue, and densely bearded, reflexed falls. Blooming even earlier is *Iris pumila atroviolacea*, or so it has always been known to me. A cute little pigmy, it is practically stemless, the flowers raised about three inches on the perianth tube above the rhizome. It is warm velvety red-purple in color, the falls a little deeper in hue than the standards. Both of these bloom in April and are indispensable in the rock garden. I particularly like these little Irises near spreads of the white or the pink common Arabis. Then there is a host of slightly taller bearded dwarfs, ranging from six to twelve inches in height and varying in color. For yellow I like Orange Queen, compact and dwarf and of a good uniform hue, also Statellae, very pale, very fragrant, and growing a foot tall. Black Midget is a good very dark purple, black as night in the bud and of dwarf stature; Socrates is a handsome wine-red, six to eight inches; Ditton Purple, dark plum color. For white there is the pretty little Bride, and there are numerous new and expensive kinds that I have not yet got round to. Many of these, however, are given glowing descriptions in catalogues that they do not quite deserve, and the wary purchaser will try to see them either in a nursery or in a botanic garden before parting with any considerable sum. The sponsors for Iris sometimes seem to have as little weakness for truth as the sponsors for tooth paste that beguile us on the air. Every two or three years these dwarf bearded Irises should be lifted and divided, and the strongest rhizomes replanted in freshly dug soil. For twenty years I have grown *Iris lurida,* a strange copperish purple bearded species, said to be native of the southeast of Europe. There is no trick to growing it, and it is effective in a somber way. Also if your garden is a hot and sunny one it will probably bloom a second time in the autumn, at which you will be properly excited and pleased.

My favorite of all the little beards, however, is *I. arenaria,* the Sand Iris. I think I had the first stock of this that ever saw the light in this country. It was raised from seed, and the seedlings planted out in a bed of almost pure sand near a south-facing wall in my old Rockland County garden. By sheer beginner's luck it was given just what it wanted, and it throve prodigiously, shooting out all over in fat exciting buds in late April, that opened into large yellow flowers, one or two to the short stem—the gayest small thing imaginable. It has a much-branched creeping rhizome, and the leaves are narrow and only two or three inches long. It is a native of Hungary, Transylvania, and the south of Russia. I've always grown this Iris since, but never have I had the success with it that I had in the hot sand of my old garden. My present garden can provide heat and sand, but there is always the horrid summer humidity and winter damp to take the heart out of it and me. It is a scarce little Iris on the American market, but it is quite easy to raise from seed—if you can get the seed. Sun and sand, remember, and something nourishing to get its roots into farther down.

That ends the little beards so far as I am concerned, and the Evansia or crested group are pushing forward for notice. These are all charmers of the first water. They are eight in number, but *japonica, Wattii, Milesii,* and *speculatrix* are of no use to us, being too tall or too tender. Even so we are left with riches, and two of them we are proud to recognize as native-born. Conspicuous features common to this group are the slender greenish rhizomes and a wavy crest along the center of the falls. These are perhaps the most wholly captivating of all Irises. Best known to most of us is probably *Iris cristata,* the charming species found along streams and on hillsides in Maryland, Ohio, Kentucky, Arkansas, and other southern-lying states. The slender rhizome is wide-creeping, the leaves narrow and when full grown six to eight inches long, the flowers large and in various tones of China blue, from deep to pale with a bright gold crest, and there is an exquisite white form. It spreads into broad masses and in early May after the Pumilas are past is alight with blooms. It likes the low sections of the rock garden, being especially lovely dipping over the brink of a pool. Or it thrives along a border edge where the soil is strong and not too dry. The white form is rather scarce and with me much less willing to abet my pride, remaining somewhat skimpy of increase. Yet for my neighbor it literally ramps in a rock garden spread out beneath high-branched deciduous trees on a hillside. A very dry situation, I should say, but apparently just to the mind of this shy beauty. In her garden it is the blue form that withholds and has to be coaxed. Such are the incalculable ways of plants that endear them to us.

A much smaller Iris that is sometimes regarded as a northerly form of *Iris cristata,* is *I. lacustris.* It is found along the shores of Lakes Huron and Superior, and while quite hardy is not always quite responsive. The flower is a fairy one, stemless and hoisted on its perianth tube to a height of two or three inches. It is China blue and half hidden among the little leaves. Along a pale streak in the center of the falls runs a white orange-tipped crest. Transplanting should be accomplished during the growing season, and the best place for this Iris is in the not-quite-dry, open sections of the rock garden, or along the edges of the pool. Both these species occasionally flower in autumn.

Iris gracilipes is a Japanese alpine and what the catalogues call a true gem for the rock garden. Many persons, I find, however, have trouble with it, but I think this is chiefly a matter of lack of understanding of its needs. What it needs, what indeed it must have, is a light slightly moist soil, richly impregnated with leaf-mold, and a situation where it does not receive the ardent rays of the sun all day. Often a stone placed at a strategic point will give it the necessary shelter, and incidentally conserve the moisture that it craves. But do not make the mistake of planting it in *wet* ground. There must be sharp drainage. The whole plant is light and airy in appearance; the leaves, green and thin in texture, are about six inches long at flowering time, the wiry stem exceeding them in length and bearing one to three fragile pinky-lilac flowers, individually fugacious but following one another in quick succession so that the plant is like a bouquet during its festive season. It blooms with me in May. Perhaps it would always be considered one of the best twenty-five rock plants. It has individuality and charm and is not too easy. I have planted it at many seasons but most successfully just after flowering. It is quite hardy in the neighborhood of New York and came through the exceptionally bitter winter of 1933–34 unscathed. A white form of it is listed, and it must be ethereally lovely; but I have not seen it.

There remains still to be mentioned in the crested group the Roof Iris, reputedly of Japan but in fact a native of China and imported therefrom to the flowery isle. It is an easily grown species asking only drainage and sunshine and most imperatively to be taken up every three years at least, pulled to pieces and replanted in new-dug soil at about midsummer. It roots very shallowly, so quickly exhausts the soil, thus requiring to be revitalized by this treatment. This is not one of the really small species, for the flowers are large and the leaves, that are broad and thin and a sort of yellowish green, are a foot in height. Among them appear on stout stems as twins or triplets the beautiful blooms. They are among the most beautiful of all Irises. Broad and flat with very short standards, they have something the appearance of a Japanese Iris, the falls drooping only a little. The color of the type is a warm heliotrope, the falls richly stained with purple. The crest is white run with gray along the top. The crest on the exquisite white form is yellow. I have raised both forms from seed many times and find that they may be counted upon to come true.

Among the smallest members of the beardless section certain ones stand out as being especially worth while. The possession of *Iris minuta* is more a matter of pride than of actual pleasure in its beauty. It is perhaps the smallest Iris, and very scarce in this country. It likes the identical conditions that suit *Iris gracilipes,* and under these conditions gives little or no trouble. My single tuft, however, never seems to grow any larger, is never large enough to make even the faint show of which it is capable. The reason is that it is one of the plants in the garden that are most eagerly coveted by visitors. I say each year firmly to myself, "I will not give away any *Iris minuta* this year—I must propagate it." And then there I am, the first thing I know, pulling off bits. But this year I positively will not, for last summer was very hard on it and it almost ceased to be, at least for me. It is a very small thing, only a few inches high with grassy leaves which rise from a compact mass of little rhizomes among which appear in early May tiny little yellow blossoms tinged with brown so fleeting as to seem almost apologetic. Mr. Dykes says it is peculiar in that nodules form on its roots as on those of leguminous plants. It is a "wee Japanese," or possibly another steal from China. Its origin seems not to be quite certain. If it were not for pride, I should not lose any sleep over this little plant.

But with another small species that I've had a hard time holding on to, it is a different story. Many years ago, at least fifteen, I raised from seed an Iris labeled *I. setosa labrador*. In due time it bloomed, and I was enchanted with it. About five inches tall over all, the blossoms of a most beguiling gray-blue, delicately etched, the standards shrunken away almost to nothing, the falls correspondingly conspicuous and broad-spreading. When massed it made a most lovely film of color. It too was coveted by visitors, and presently I was reduced to one little clump; then came the exodus from the old garden, and I lost my ewe lamb. I mourned and mourned in print and out. It pays to advertise your horticultural griefs, believe me, for gardeners are generous and sympathetic. One day Mr. Clarence Sutcliffe of Poughkeepsie sent me a nice bit of *I. setosa labrador,* which he said he had had from his uncle Mr. Clarence Lown, who had had it from me originally. A happy reunion that. In the meantime I had raised from seed all sorts of *setosas,* some under the name of *s. canadensis,* some called *Hookeri,* some called *tridentata.* No *labrador* could I find, and none of the impersonators had the dwarf form nor the special tender quality of blueness, though all were nice enough if one had not seen the original.

Then there was the sad tale of *Iris ruthenica,* which also, I hasten to say, had a happy ending. Any one seeing its portrait in Mr. Dykes' great book, "The

Little Irises

Genus Iris," would be intrigued as was I. But it could
not be bought in our quarantine-locked country. Nor
could I find seed of it. Finally an Irish seedhouse
offered the seed. I ordered it, planted it, and fertilized
it with prayers. Three stingy little wisps were the
result. These were petted and cosseted by me and
seemed to respond. But one day I took my eye momen-
tarily off the by-the-day man. When I replaced it, I
met a beaming Latin glance. "I cleana up disa place,"
he said with happy if misplaced certainty of praise.
Well, those three waifs had gone to limbo. We could
not find them though we spent three dollars and sixty
cents' worth of predepression time searching in places
where Angelo, now cast down and penitent, thought he
might have thrown them. Years went by, seeds were
secured more than once and hopefully raised but always resulted in some gawky stalwart. And then one
shining April day out of the Northwest, like any jaunty
young Lochinvar, came *Iris ruthenica,* like a homing
pigeon. (My mixed metaphors are due to reminiscent
excitement.) The plant came, I must state, from the
nursery of Mr. Carl Starker at Jennings Lodge, Oregon,
who often has up his sleeve the very thing you've been
pining for. It settled down at once to contentment,
this plant, weathered the record winter of 1933–34,
and now, fat and tufty, is preparing to bloom. Such are
the great moments in a gardener's life. And now I'll
tell you what it will be like. The blossoms will be borne
on short stems and about two inches in diameter, bright
purple with a tinge of red on the standards, and the
falls daintily penciled with white. It is a native of
Russia and Siberia. When you get it, give it a position

in full sun on the slope of a rock garden where the soil is light and good, but well drained.

There remains of the small beardless Irises *I. verna,* that scrambles over railway embankments, sand hills, along roadsides in the acid, sandy barrens of the southern states. I have seen it in mats many yards wide in North Carolina, covering the most forbidding sand with its lovely sparkling blooms. It is one of the gayest of the small Irises. The flower held erectly on its very short stem is bright purple, and running from below the apex of the blade down the claw is a gaudy golden streak flanked with white. The leaves grow six inches high and persist through the winter. The rhizome is moderately stout and creeping. *Iris verna* adds to its other charms a lovely fragrance. I call *I. verna* a fussy plant because it does not thrive for me. My neighbor Herbert Durand, however, grows it in a manner to make the eyes bulge and the heart swell with envy. Though we have discovered that many of the dictums about acid-loving plants can be discarded as so many notions, I suspect that this is one which really requires it. Anyway, I have never seen it well grown save in a sandy acid medium. Sun and partial shade seem alike to it.

Two bulbous Irises grow here and are both forms of the same species. They are the earliest Irises to flower here—usually in late April. *Iris reticulata,* suddenly appearing like a gorgeous purple and gold jeweled beetle thrusting upwards between stiff, four-sided, horned leaves, is always a surprise. Its brilliance fairly holds one spellbound, while its violet fragrance ravishes the nose. I have just been looking at my cherished patch, which is the result of careful husbanding of a handful of bulbs given me many years ago. Also I have been looking it up in domestic and foreign catalogues and find it listed here at two dollars the small netted bulb, while just across the water, which grows narrower all the time, indeed just across the border, it is to be had for a few shillings the hundred. Morals could be drawn and tales adorned—but it would be a useless waste of paper and ink.

Iris reticulata is so desirable as to come under the head of a necessity. It is not difficult to grow once you have it and once you understand that heat and light and drainage are imperative to its well-being. My patch flourishes on a little plain against a large south-facing stone in the rock garden. Once I was so reckless as to take up a few bulbs and bring them indoors. They flowered perfectly and went back into the ground seemingly none the worse for the adventure. Once in several years we dig up the bulbs carefully after the foliage has lengthened out and ripened, redig the soil, and replant them, giving them a little more room and rejoicing in the modest increase.

Iris reticulata Krelagei has the advantage of blossoming two weeks in advance of its relative, but there the advantage ceases. In color it is a rather unpleasing red-purple, and it has no beguiling fragrance. Both come from the neighborhood of the Caucasus. There are other forms of *I. reticulata*—*histrio, histrioides, cyanea, humilis, sophenensis*—but though I now and then think I am on the track of them I do not come up with them.

The sole Juno Iris that I grow, I sometimes think is

the loveliest flower in the garden. This is *Iris persica,* an old flower in European gardens. I hesitate to try to describe it, for no words beaten out on the keys of a typewriter could do it justice. The bulb is ovoid and nearly as large as a hen's egg. The leaves are narrow and four or five in a tuft. The single flower borne on a very short stem is large—two to three inches across—and tops the leaves. The color is strange and exquisite—a sort of pallid sea-green, almost white, yet with the suggestion of green strong. Blackish purple patches set it off, a streak of orange—no use, it must be seen. It flowers just after *Iris reticulata* and comes from Asia Minor and Persia. I have perhaps half a dozen bulbs. They do not all flower every year. The season when three appear I think myself lucky. Like *I. reticulata* it wants a hot, well drained situation and to be baked in summer. Mr. Dykes inclines towards a fairly heavy soil for it. I do not take issue with him, but mine are growing in the ordinary rock garden mixture; and when they produce flowers they do it heartily and are perfect, while in England they are said to behave miffily. There are other forms of *Iris persica* that sound utterly lovely, but what use to think of them? I close this chapter on a note of discontent. Why may we not have easily and lawfully these small jeweled Irises? What harm could they do? Whose bank account would be seriously jeopardized by their admission to our shores? Here is a work for the garden clubs to do; a worthy fight to be waged.

CHAPTER VII

In AND about a fairly spacious rock garden, as well as in the garden borders, there is every reason to make use of some of the taller Iris species. These that I am going to name are not as tall as many of the *sibirica* group as *aurea* or *Monnieri, ochroleuca* or the *spurias,* but they are taller than those named in the preceding chapter. Nor do they bulk and mass as do the showy members of the bearded group. They are slender, with grasslike foliage and lightly made blossoms that seem to float above them like butterflies. They are, so it seems to me, in the spirit of the rock garden, whereas the heavier bearded kinds very distinctly are not. Many of them are exquisite and bear the minutest inspection, and none is really difficult to grow. In the rock garden they supply height or stability where it is needed, but they must not be set up in competition with the true dwarfs; they should be given situations on the outskirts of the rock garden or at strategic points where they will contrast with some rampant spreader such as Arabis, hardy Candytuft, or *Phlox subulata.* They belong to the beardless section, or to what are known as the apogon Irises. It would be a great pity to allow our interest in the bearded species to blind us to the beauty and merit of their less known sisters. The majority of them prefer rather low situations—that is rather moist soil, not the bone-dry heights. And all these named are easily come by.

To take them alphabetically we have first:

Iris bulleyana. This is a handsome species supposedly but not certainly from western China and not very old in gardens, for it has but recently appeared on the Iris horizon, and I have not heard that its exact origin is known. The hollow stem grows to a height of about eighteen inches, carrying the wide blossoms just above the grasslike leaves. They are deep lilac as to the standards, while the falls are cream-colored, closely veined with bluish purple. There will be some variation in the color of the flowers of plants raised from seed. This species prefers a well-drained dampish situation.

Iris chrysographes is unique and beautiful. It is another plant from western China, this one introduced by Mr. Wilson in recent times. The blossoms are a rich dark red-violet, almost black in some forms, and they are handsomely and conspicuously veined on the haft with gold. It grows eighteen inches tall. I have not found this an easy plant to satisfy; its stem is hollow, proclaiming its pleasure in moisture, but it has proved with me a poor doer, increasing slowly and in some seasons refusing to bloom. This is doubtless due to some fault in its care or feeding, as I have heard no complaint of it from other sources. *I. Chrysofor* is an attractive hybrid between the foregoing and *I. Forrestii.* It displays a good deal of variety in different individuals, some showing pretty combinations of blue and yellow, others having white, lavender, purple or bronzy-yellow blossoms. The habit is that of a dwarf *sibirica* with masses of very slender foliage. The flowers are good for cutting and last for several days in water.

Iris Clarkei (*I. himalaica*) is a member of this same group and comes from high in the Himalaya Mountains. The stem is solid, though otherwise closely resembling the *sibiricas,* and it will stand a dryer situation. The flowers are variable from blue to purple, and the falls are long and drooping. Occasionally the flowers have yellow markings.

Iris dichotoma, the Vesper Iris, takes us clear away from the type of the above Irises. It is the sole member of its section, the pardanthopsis section, and is unique on more than one count. In the first place it blossoms in August, and then, as its common name implies, it flowers towards evening, when it sends forth a delicate fragrance. It is a freely branching slender plant, the forked flowering stems growing to a height of about two feet. The leaves, which do not reach the height of the stems, are set in the form of a fan. The Vesper Iris is very floriferous; the small flowers are borne in racemes, and while individually fugacious continue to appear over a considerable period. The flowers give the effect of being gray-blue; but there is some variation, and last summer I saw in the nursery of P. J. van Melle, at Poughkeepsie, New York, a fine white form. I have since procured seed, and as the seedlings are now up in the frames I am hoping to have this attractive albino in my garden soon. Seed, by the way, is freely produced by this Iris and germinates easily. I have found the plants very short-lived individually; in fact they often bloom themselves to death the first year. In

Horticulture, however, Roderick M. Crockett, of Cranford, New Jersey, writes, "There is no question that this charming Iris is hardy and can perpetuate itself by offsets from the meager base, though it exhausts itself considerably in the flowering process." Mr. Crockett also reports that his plants have self-sown freely, which mine have not as yet done; but in any case seed is so freely produced, and the seedlings grow so rapidly that there is no trick about keeping this pretty Vesper flower about the garden. It comes originally from Siberia and northern China and does not demand a damp situation—rather, I should say, the reverse. It is growing here at the back of a low mound in the rock garden and seems comfortably situated.

Iris ensata is a Japanese that I raised many years ago from seed. It has one outstanding characteristic that sometimes makes it an embarrassment. Once rooted and grown into a good clump in a situation that is to its mind, it is almost impossible to remove should the occasion arise. It anchors itself with thoroughness and determination, and I have more than once had to resort to my invaluable small trench pick and an arm considerably more muscular than mine to dislodge it. Otherwise it is a pretty and desirable species, making a mass of tough narrow leafage through which, and not topping it, in early May appear myriads of gray-lavender butterfly flowers, the standards and falls of which are very narrow, airy, and charming and exquisitely veined with white. After the flowering is over the leaves elongate and reflex somewhat. It is necessary in placing this Iris to remember that though your young specimen may appear so slight it will grow steadily more rotund, and it is best to allow for this increase in girth in the beginning or be prepared to resort to drastic methods of removal at no very distant date. Mr. Dykes says this Iris seems to abound everywhere in central Asia and northern China. I've found no situation in the garden where it was not perfectly willing to grow, and it self-sows, sometimes inconveniently.

Iris foliosa is a beautiful native species found from Kentucky to Kansas. It should not properly be grown in a rock garden, for the blossoms, which are of the texture of velvet and a rich royal purple, are too large in scale. But I can never resist it. It seems to me one of the most beautiful of its beautiful race. The stem is crooked to a height of eighteen inches; the leaves are taller and somewhat lax. I grow it in a little border near the rock garden, where its roots can wander about freely, and it is only when the blossoms are in evidence that I permit myself a glance at this rather untidy corner. It is quite hardy.

Iris Forrestii is a charming Iris that might be described as a dwarf yellow-flowered *sibirica*. It was introduced from high altitudes in western China by Mr. Forrest and is a valuable garden plant. The flowers are a good clear tone of yellow, occasionally veined; the falls, long and graceful, are carried well above the slender leaves. This species thrives in any well made border or in low sections of the rock garden. It is especially well placed near a little pool.

Iris fulva (*I. cuprea*), from swamps in the southeastern states, is quite unique among Irises as to color —a rich terra-cotta; and the blossoms have a curiously drooping effect. It grows from two to three feet tall and seems, in spite of its southern origin, to be quite hardy in the neighborhood of New York. But it is not always an easy species to flower. The best success I have had with it was in a bed of black soil brought from a swamp. The soil was not wet but was, of course, naturally retentive of a certain amount of moisture. In this it grew and flowered freely every year. An interesting hybrid has been raised between *I. fulva* and *I. hexagona,* another southern species, which retains the large velvety flowers of the latter and takes a slightly coppery tone from the former. It is found in catalogues as *Iris fulvala.* It is a good doer in ordinary rich soil and full sun.

Iris graminea is sometimes called the Plum Iris because to some noses its flowers have the fragrance of ripe plums. This species belongs to central and southern Europe and to the Caucasus, but it has been in cultivation as a garden flower for more than two hundred years. It is a pretty little species, though not showy, for the blossoms hide away among the abundant tufts of grasslike leaves. These grow little more than a foot in height. The flowers are small, profusely borne and of a pretty red-purple, marked with white. Any fair situation in the rock garden or borders satisfies it completely, though it prefers sunshine. It is not too tall for use in the rock garden though it must be kept in mind that it increases in girth rather rapidly, which must be allowed for, or the plant taken up and divided occasionally. The fragrance seems not to be a fixed characteristic, for in a batch of seedlings some will be totally lacking in scent. Brought into the house with plenty of its slender leaves and placed in a low bowl, this little Iris never fails to attract favorable comment.

Iris hexagona is a southern species whose blossoms are rather large in scale for the rock garden, and it seems to try to hide them away among its abundant lax foliage. It comes from swamps in South Carolina, Florida, and Texas but has proved quite hardy and indestructible here in this garden for many years, and self-sows with great freedom. Also it is growing in a dry situation with a southern exposure and seems entirely content, so swamp life is not necessary to it. The flowers are very blue and appear in May. Mr. Dykes cites this as one of the species very difficult to flower in England.

Iris longipetala is a lovely flower of the Californian coastal district. It is one of the few Californians that are fairly easy to deal with. This is probably due to the fact that it will grow in calcareous or neutral soils, while most of the Californians demand acidity. It blooms in May, the stem rising to a height of two feet, the blossoms large with clear lavender standards and gray-white falls, veined with deep violet.

Iris missouriensis (*I. Tolmieana, I. longipetala montana*). This is a rather widely distributed species in the Far West. It bears pale lavender-blue flowers on fifteen-inch stems in May. The foliage is of about the same length. Left to itself in rather heavy soil that is moist, or kept moist during the growing season, it forms heavy clumps; but it resents disturbance and should not be moved unless it shows by poor growth or lack of blossoms that it is not happily situated. There are some fine forms of this Iris offered by

What Happens in My Garden

D. M. Andrews, notably Bluebird and Snowbird, the flowers of the latter pure white with no veining and the plant somewhat dwarfer than the type.

Iris prismatica. Our common native eastern species, *Iris versicolor*, is too pervasive and strong-growing to allow anywhere near the rock garden, but with *I. prismatica* the case is quite different. This is one of my favorite Irises, a most graceful and engaging species that grows none too plentifully in moist meadows of the eastern states. Its stems, curiously wiry and branching, rise to a height of about eighteen inches, and the sprightly flowers are in tones of blue and violet lightly marked with yellow. I rescued my plants from a neighboring marshy meadow some years ago. Now neat streets cross and recross its playground and prim little houses rise where once its blue flowers reproduced the sky. I am glad I saved them from their seemingly inevitable fate.

Iris Wilsoni. With this species we return to China. It somewhat resembles *I. Forrestii* but is a slightly taller and heavier plant. The flowers are yellow, the standards pale and lightly veined with purple, the falls deeper and netted with brown at the throat. It likes a damp situation and rich soil. It is said to grow three feet high, but I have never known it to reach this height. Altogether it is a less attractive plant to my thinking than *I. Forrestii.*

There is no doubt of the fact the Californian and other northwestern species of Iris offer an incentive to the rock gardener to solve the problem of their culture in the East. Very possibly it has been solved, but I have heard nothing that seems to me very conclusive. It is thought by many authorities that the time for planting them is when they are in full growth, yet the most successful plantings I have made were in the very late autumn. To raise them from seed is undoubtedly the surest method of securing them, for the babies are more easily acclimated than the full-grown specimens. Seed is easily procured fresh, and seedlings commonly flower in two years. A sandy acid soil is generally recommended for them, and sun for at least a part of the day. The foliage of many of them remains green over the winter, and the fact that this is sometimes killed off in our severe winters may account for some of the mortality. I had a thriving colony of *I. tenax* for a number of years but lost it entirely during this past excessively cold winter. Some lovely kinds are *I. tenax, I. Douglasiana, I. bracteata, I. tenuis,* a charming white-flowered form from Oregon; and there are a number of others. Any western dealer will furnish a list worth getting acquainted with.

CHAPTER VIII

FLAXFLOWERS

THERE are in the garden, as in the world of human beings, individuals who make a great noise, who occupy much space, who count definitely and solidly in the general scheme of things. They are important—necessary in fact—in both spheres. But there are also whimsical, light-hearted persons (or plants) who diffuse a gentle gaiety from odd corners, and who achieve grace and subtlety in unconsidered situations; and their mission is as important if less definite. In the first category, speaking now wholly of the garden, belong the Phloxes, the Delphiniums, the Helianthuses, the Hollyhocks. In the second, among others, belong the Flaxflowers, or to give them their proper name, the Linums. The garden would be a poor place indeed without their type.

The Linums belong to the order Linaceae and comprise some eighty species of annual, biennial, and perennial herbs and shrubs that abound in all the temperate regions of the earth but are rare in the tropics. Only a tithe of these are in cultivation, a very few in general cultivation.

As I have said, there is nothing solid or serious about these plants; they are airy, graceful, fugitive in their blossoming, and in my experience even the certified

[64]

hardy perennials among them are short-lived. They give their best display in the first two seasons after being raised from seed; after that the plants seemingly become debilitated and discouraged and usually die off. Seed, however, is freely borne and freely self-sown, so that once you have them, unless you are of those meticulous old-maidish gardeners who cannot bear a petal or plant out of place, you are likely always to have plenty of sturdy young seedlings springing up about the garden. Just so they come readily from hand-sown seed consigned to a cold frame in late November or to a well prepared seedbed in the early spring.

I should not want a garden without plenty of these airy Flaxflowers of one kind and another fluttering forth to meet the genial warmth of early summer days. They have a gentle but persuasive charm, once you begin to know them, that leads you on to become acquainted with one member of the family after another. The common Flax of commerce is *Linum usitatissimum,* that has been in cultivation so long that the place of its origin has been lost sight of. It is seldom cultivated in gardens but is widely naturalized in Europe and elsewhere. One wonders whether Longfellow had seen it when he penned the line, "Blue were her eyes as the fairy-flax," or if he was drawing on his poetic imagination.

Blue indeed is the color we most usually associate with these flowers, for *Linum perenne* is the species most frequently met with in gardens; and its round flowers, opening only in sunshine and lasting not much beyond midday, are so numerous and so blue as to make their short daily appearance truly memorable. As a matter of fact, however, there are pure white Flaxflowers, as well as mauve and rose and bright yellow ones.

Most of the Linums are little fussy about the quality of soil in which they grow, provided it is impeccably drained, and that the sun reaches them freely; for they all resent damp feet and are the most ardent sun lovers. There is a certain neatness of habit about even the taller kinds that recommends them for use in the rock garden, as well as along the edges of sunny, well drained borders. There is too what might be termed a sturdy delicacy about them; they look fragile but are not. Winds bend but do not break them, storms dash against their slenderness with little effect. I have not found the tallest of them to require staking. Their love of sure drainage predisposes them in favor of gravel paths as a dwelling place and they make the most charming and least obtrusive of squatters.

To begin with the blue-flowered kinds, *Linum perenne* is the one most often grown. It is a hardy perennial belonging to Europe and blossoming from mid-May (about New York) through June and into July. The wiry stems arise fountainlike from the somewhat narrow leaves, bearing at the top a cluster of bright but soft blue flowers, round as pennies, that open with the first light of morning, long before most of us are stirring, and scatter a blue carpet about the plants soon after midday. They grow something over a foot in height. If, when flowering is over, the plants are cut back to about six inches, new growth will be encouraged, and a new crop of flowers probably produced.

Flaxflowers

This is a charming and beguiling plant for use anywhere in the garden, whether set to wave its delicate stems from a height in the rock garden or to confound the fat respectability of the habitual border dwellers.

The white-flowered form, *L. perenne album,* is also a lovely thing, though less often seen. I once had a mass planting of it against a low wall that was veiled with gray Cerastium. This made a delightful picture. Once also I planted a broad edge of the blue form along a wide border intermingled with the bright Spanish Poppy, *Papaver rupifragum,* and May-flowering Tulips in tones of lavender. This gave a long flowering, for though the Tulips were soon over the Flax and the apricot-hued Poppies continued for many weeks. Bits of low pea brush were inserted along the edge, and the branches of the Flax drawn down to create a shower effect that was very pretty.

Considered by many to be even more desirable than *Linum perenne* is *L. narbonnense,* native of southern Europe, and differing from the above in being slightly taller, the flowers slightly larger and bluer in spite of a delicate line of other color down each petal. It is less fugacious also than *L. perenne* and, according to Clarence Elliott, if picked just before it opens, lasts well in water. From its southern habitat it might be thought tender, but it has proved quite hardy here, though it is certainly not long-lived. *Linum Lewisi,* from our West country, I once grew in the rock garden and found distinctly inferior to either of the foregoing, though a good deal like them. Its blue is less definite, its height greater, and its habit less graceful. Save in a collection, I think it is not worth growing.

But *Linum austriacum* is a delightful free-flowering species for the rock garden, with substantial bright blue flowers and a fountain of stems of no great height, not usually more than nine inches. This is perhaps a better plant than the dainty little *L. alpinum,* standing erect where the latter sprays about over the surrounding stones, each six-inch stem bearing a cluster of large soft blue salvers. *L. collinum* is a species akin to these that is found in the mountains of Greece; it is very lovely and blooms most of the summer. Make a planting on a sunny, rocky hillside of the rock garden of any of these little mountain Flaxes and interplant them closely with the Alpine Poppy in tones of pink and buff and scarlet, and enjoy a dream of fair flowers that will give you exquisite pleasure for many weeks in the early summer.

It should be borne in mind that these mountain Flaxes require a really poor and half-starved soil if they are to maintain their dwarf, compact character, and that they quite definitely like lime in their diet. All require to be planted in generous numbers also if they are to prove their beauty and worth conclusively. It is well, too, to remember that like all the race they are taprooted and exceedingly resent disturbance. Therefore seedlings should be moved to permanent quarters when very small.

In high, dry pastures and on towering limestone hills of southern Europe is found *L. salsoloides,* sometimes called the pearl of the race, but to my mind in no way comparable to the little blue-flowered kinds just enumerated. As in the case of so many of its kind, its rootstock is woody, the slender wiry stems pushing up fountain-wise and clothed in narrow stiffish leaves set very close together. The salver-shaped flowers are white veined with deeper color, and I have seen a form with a purplish blotch at the base of each petal. It forms a little low bush suitable for a hot sunny place in the rock garden. A dwarf form of it is sometimes listed as *L. salsoloides nanum* and sometimes as *L. tenuifolium*. This is lauded as a very fine rock plant, but I have to confess that I have not been successful with it; that is, it has always failed to materialize the "dense fur-like mats almost hidden under the hundreds of opalescent white flowers" attributed to it and has persisted with me in being rather scant and straggly and altogether unconvincing of any special loveliness. *L. viscosum* I have not grown. It belongs, I believe, to the taller section of the Flaxflowers, sending up few or even single stems, rather sticky, crowned with a cluster of rose-purple flowers. Mr. Farrer says it has "a stalwart and quite unflaxlike effectiveness," and that because of its "lignescent unfibred root" it is difficult to transplant, but once established is a reliable perennial. It is offered in this country.

Linum monogynum, that makes the most delightful filmy little bushes imaginable, neat and compact and about a foot in height, is said to be covered for most of the summer with large gleaming white blossoms. These I have never seen, for though I have more than once conjured the little bushes into being from a packet of seed I have not been able to carry them over the winter. This is not to say definitely that they are not hardy, but only that I have so far failed to provide these New Zealanders with the proper amount of heat

and light and perfect drainage that they must have in
order to weather our inclement winters. All who have
grown it agree as to its worth-whileness. A packet of
seed costs little, and success may be lurking just around
the corner; so it is again on the seed list.

The yellow-flowered Flaxes, so far as I know them,
are quite different in appearance from any that we have
mentioned. They have their own individuality and
charm but are more substantial in leaf and stalk and
flower, for the most part good herbaceous plants for
the border or rock garden that die back to a thick
rootstock annually. *Linum flavum* is well known for its
fine display of rich yellow flowers in early summer. It
grows about a foot tall, but with me is not a good
stayer, not so good nor so showy a plant as *Linum
campanulatum*, which Mr. Farrer says cannot be separated from the foregoing. *L. capitatum*, introduced
from Austria a little more than a hundred years ago,
is also a fine yellow-flowered form close to *L. flavum*,
but with the blossoms set in a closer head. None of
these is perhaps very long-lived; therefore it is well to
raise them occasionally from seed to insure their per-
manence in the garden. *L. arboreum*, the so-called Tree
Flax, is not a tree but a quaint little bushling from high
places in the island of Crete, evergreen, and comely
with fine large yellow blossoms; but with me it does
not prove hardy.

Those who have devoured the pages of Mr. Farrer's
"English Rock Garden" have perhaps come upon the
coveted little yellow-flowered Flax thus described:
"*Linum aretioeides* is perhaps the most to be desired
of all. It makes a quite tight small mass of leafage,

narrow, fine, frail, and huddled so that the whole looks exactly like a cushion of *Douglasia vitaliana;* in which, however, sit stemless the flaming cups of gold, each by itself as the similar cushions of *Geranium nivalis,"* and so on. But where is this jewel of the "mountain region of Cadmus in Caria and Tmolus in Lydia" to be found? It has been in no seed list that I have ever seen: I seek it still in vain. It is perhaps such apparently hopeless quests that give gardening its peculiar zest. But I should like to find it!

To return to level ground and the easily attainable, the so-called Scarlet Flax, a hardy annual, may be had by any one. And if a succession of sowings is made from early spring every two weeks, its ruby-colored salvers may be enjoyed in the garden the summer and autumn through. This is *Linum grandiflorum;* it is said that there are rose and white and pale blue forms of it, but I have not seen them. This native of Algeria is a valuable border annual, doing efficient work in lightening the heavier effects of border upholstery, and if young plants are potted up in the autumn they continue their cheerful display in the greenhouse or conservatory.

Less well known is a little annual Flax that is said to be frequently met with in the Alps and sub-Alps of Europe, western Asia, and the Canary Islands. This is *L. catharcticum.* It has little oblong leaves and small white flowers. I grew it long ago upon a sunny slope of the rock garden. While it was pleasant enough for one season, I did not think it quite worth repeating.

CHAPTER IX

BEAUTY IN ONIONS

A NIMBLE-WITTED person once said that if Onions did not already exist they would have to be invented. This, of course, was the pronouncement of an epicure, a gourmet, and he had in mind those members of the tribe that have gastronomic importance, not especially those possessed of sufficient beauty to give them flower garden value. And in truth no lover of good eating would willingly do away with the Shallot (*Allium ascalonicum*), the Garlic (*A. sativum*), Chives (*A. Schoenoprasum*), or even the humble Onion itself (*A. Cepa*), or the still humbler Leek (*A. Porrum*). But none of these have any part in the decorative scheme of the garden, unless it be Chives that have so quaint an attractiveness, thrifty and neat, of their own, that one might find a less personable edging for a bed or a nook in the rock garden. They offer more spiritual attractions than their flavorous leaves in their profusely borne heads of rosy-lilac flowers.

The genus Allium belongs to the natural order Liliaceae and comprises three hundred species, or thereabouts, widely distributed over the temperate regions of the Northern Hemisphere. They are of the easiest culture in any open place, or along the edge of woodland in light soil, naturalizing happily in the wild gar-

[72]

den and consorting effectively with certain Ferns. The different kinds flower over a period covering the late spring and summer, the blossoms borne in round heads or loose clusters, white, yellow, blue, or in tones of mauve or rose. Most of them increase rapidly from offsets or self-sown seed, often by both methods.

Many of them, it must be confessed, are indefensible weeds that should on no account be admitted to the garden, but others have real beauty and decorative value, and even those that are prone to sow themselves too freely may be kept in check if the flower heads are removed before the seed matures and is scattered. All the species are quite easily raised from seed, so if we are unable to buy bulbs of the kinds we covet we need not necessarily forgo them on that account.

Our own country is rich in Allium species, and while some are of the genus weed, and to be avoided, others are extremely pretty. *A. cernuum,* the Allegheny Onion, and *A. stellatum,* the Prairie Onion, found on rocky slopes from Minnesota to Montana, have grown in my garden for many years. The first is the prettier, the stems growing about eighteen inches high and bearing aloft a loose cluster of drooping pale lavender flowers, like ornaments done in delicate enamel. *A. stellatum* has a broader head of flowers and is rosier in color and distinctly less choice in appearance. Both are easy and pervasive and should not be suffered in the choicer regions of the rock garden, but are very suitable for the wild garden, or to grow along a woodland path. *A. acuminatum* is another pretty species from the Northwest, with deep rose-colored flowers, almost an inch across, in a many-flowered umbel on a nine-inch stem, appearing in summer.

A choice little American Allium is *A. Bidwelliae,* found in the Sierra Nevada. It is a dwarf member of the clan admirably suited to the rock garden as it grows only three or four inches high, bearing its few-flowered umbel of soft rosy flowers in July. Another very choice rock garden kind is *A. cyaneum,* a charming dwarf perhaps six inches high over all, making a little bush of grasslike leaves out of which the slender stems hoist loose heads of blue flowers in July and August. It hails from the Altai Mountains and is quite hardy. Akin to this are two other most attractive little species, *A. kansuense* and *A. sikkimense,* both very dwarf and very pretty, with little to choose between them. There is some confusion between these Tibetan Alliums, and seed may not yield just what you expect—but so much the more entertaining.

A. Beesianum, a very distinctive kind, with loose heads of fragile, fringed, bell-shaped flowers, an unusual China blue in color, amidst its grasslike foliage, is also suitable for the rock garden as it grows no more than nine or ten inches high and has a really choice appearance. It has another virtue also, that of blooming late, in August and September. It is a western China species.

Allium Moly, a Spanish woodland species, called in Europe the Lily Leek, grows along the outskirts of my rock garden in the less choice situations. It may perhaps be a bit coarse and invasive for the company it finds there, but I admire greatly its broad, glaucous leaves and its compact bright yellow flower-heads that appear in May and make a very pretty show. So far it has not increased beyond my patience, and though so old and tried a plant in European gardens it is unaccountably scarce in this country. It is hardy and indestructible and grows according to environment from a foot to eighteen inches high. It has not self-sown with me, but the bulbs make a steady increase.

Possible for the extensive rock garden, as well as for the border, are *A. karataviense* and *A. caeruleum* (*A. azureum*). The first has two very wide glaucous leaves out of which arise in May short stout stems ending in large balls of bloom, a mass of stars of a bright reddish purple. It is from Turkestan. *A. caeruleum* is taller, a charming species with globose heads of bright blue flowers on stems perhaps fifteen inches high and triangular leaves six to nine inches tall. It blooms in late spring or early summer.

And then there is the great mass of taller as well as dwarf Alliums among which it is difficult to choose. Persons making extensive trials of these plants may elect to throw out a great many kinds as unfit for garden use or not meeting their fastidious approval, but many of them are sure to be retained. Really lovely among them is *A. neapolitanum,* from southern Europe, which unfortunately has proved not quite hardy with me, but would doubtless winter safely south of Philadelphia and on Long Island. It is called the Daffodil Garlic, and bears large heads of pure white flowers on tallish slender stems in May amidst grassy foliage. Those who wish to try it in cold climates should plant the bulbs in a warm and sheltered place in light and sandy soil.

Very attractive also is *A. narcissiflorum* (*A. pedemontanum*), the Narcissus-flowered Garlic, which hails from the "stony screes high up in the most awesome shelves of the limestone Alps of Piedmont (and far away into the Caucasus)." Here it grows into a "jungle" of erect strap-shaped leaves, among which arise in summer "springy stems of eight or ten inches, each hanging out a loose head of some six or eight flowers of a glowing vinous red. Unfortunately an evil Godmother has dowered this beauty with a commensurate drawback in the form of an exaggerated stench—a stench so horrible that one can hardly bear to collect it."

A. Ostrowskianum is also extremely handsome, "a beauty from the Alps of Turkestan," blooming at midsummer, and bearing umbels of purple-red flowers of a curiously smooth texture. It is considered about the best of the genus from a decorative standpoint, neat in habit, hardy, a low grower, which makes it suitable for the rock garden—a genuinely desirable species. Some one has suggested growing it under carpeting plants through which it will shoot upwards with pleasing effect. Closely allied to it is *A. oreophilum*, very dwarf, only three inches or so high, with two flat narrow recurving little leaves between which the rounded heads of big purple blossoms are lifted in July. I have not grown this kind, which comes from the screes of the Caucasus and Daghestan at some seven or eight thousand feet up, but it sounds desirable.

Allium triquetum is a British weed, but a very pretty one, found on cool shaded banks and moist places generally, where the dead-white bell-shaped flowers dangling above the leaves are at home and effective among such semi-savage things as *Dicentra eximia,* Harebells, and *Anemone canadense.*

And this is only a beginning. There are still of real attractiveness, *A. sphaerocephalum,* with handsome dense-flowered heads of rich crimson in July and August on stems two feet tall; *A. albidum,* with close umbels of white flowers with a conspicuous pink ovary, from Siberia; *A. flavum,* a foot-high, slender-growing species "with round, but not hollow leaves," and yellow bell-shaped flowers borne in umbels during the summer, an old garden plant and desirable, though, as it comes from Italy, to be treated with some consideration; *A. giganteum,* a rare and conspicuous species with immense globe-shaped heads of bright lilac flowers on stems four and a half feet tall in midsummer, and broad leaves close to the ground, probably the tallest of the species; and *A. albopilosum,* new and reputedly lovely with globular heads measuring eight inches across, packed with large star-shaped gleaming lilac flowers carried on stout stems eighteen inches high above downy, strap-shaped foliage. This is from northern Persia and is probably the largest-flowered of the race. It comes into flower in June and lasts in perfection for a considerable time. And still there are *A. Purdomii,* a comely little Tibetan with cluster heads of violet-blue flowers and rushlike foliage, that grows only some three or four inches high and is therefore a candidate for the rock garden; a handsome species from Bokhara, *A. Rosenbachianum,* as tall as the former is dwarf (four feet) with large globular heads of lilac flowers, something in the way of *A. giganteum,* but less brilliant, flowering in June and July: and *A. pulchellum*, that blooms in midsummer, growing two feet high with pink flower heads atop slender but erect stems, from the Orient. This for the wild garden.

This is but the merest tabulation of a few Allium possibilities. Any one starting out as we have done here to make something of a study of the genus will find much of interest and much to puzzle over. The genus is large, many of the types approximate others closely, many are good for nothing but to be cast out. But a few really fine things emerge, and we shall have more to say about them in another place.

CHAPTER X

VARIOUS members of the Daisy tribe furnish what might be called the pack horses of the garden—that is, they bear a heavy burden and one for which they seldom receive sufficient credit. We are, instead, rather inclined to look down upon these willing servitors; they are easy to grow, they ask so little—which instead of arousing our gratitude seems to engender a faint contempt. Most of us are prone to like and desire the plants that give us a little trouble, that necessitate the exercise of our wits and skill. Thus we take the easy-going Composites for granted, seldom troubling to acknowledge the very real debt we owe them for their solid usefulness.

Where, indeed, should we be without the Sunflowers, the Zinnias, the Marigolds, Cosmos, Rudbeckias, Heleniums, Pyrethrums, Boltonias, Michaelmas Daisies, Coreopsis, and the like, that make up so much of the effectiveness of our gardens, especially in the summer and autumn? Of course the Compositae have a bad name as weeds, and justly, for some of the worst and most ubiquitous of the latter are of this clan; but nevertheless we should certainly not be blinded to the genuine worth of those numerous species of which it

[79]

may well be said that when they are good they are very, very good, indeed.

Some of these play an important part in the rock garden, taking upon themselves the task of clothing in cheerful greenery and often lovely color the less desirable situations therein, and asking little help or solicitude from us in return for what they give. This ease of culture, however, while being a general rule is not an invariable one. Now and again one meets with "Daisies" that are unresponsive, even to the point of positive stand-offishness. This I have been sorry to find the case with that enchanting small creature of our Great Plains, *Townsendia escarpa*, the Easter Daisy, that makes a little tuft of dusty leaves in the midst of which sits inscrutable and impish a large pinkish flower with a gold eye on a stem that is almost no stem at all. Perfectly hardy it undoubtedly is, but it as certainly would rather die (and does invariably) than live in my garden, whatever may be my pains to make it comfortable. And this applies to the only other Townsendia that I have sought to fascinate—*T. Wilcoxiana*, with large lavender flowers. And there are others. *T. florifer*, says Ira Gabrielson, is a real beauty, and *T. incana*, from the Rockies, "is a beautifully silvered canescent species with big lilac flowers." Dr. Gabrielson soothes one's sense of failure with these aristocrats of the Compositae by saying that they are for the most part short-lived perennials or biennials, or bloom themselves to death (we hope in an excess of eagerness to please) the first season after transplantation from the wild. Raising them from seed and so inuring them from earliest youth to our conditions is probably one way of getting around their capriciousness. In any case one person's failure is not conclusive, and these small Townsendias are worth striving for.

And while we are dealing with aristocrats we might mention certain of that great and often weedy family of Erigeron. These, like the Asters to which they bear a resemblance, boast a number of choice small things for inclusion in a collection of rock plants. The colors of the Fleabanes run from white through pink to the lilacs and purples with a few yellow species, the flowers having more than one row of narrow rays and a yellow disc. The prettiest Erigeron I ever grew came to me as *E. trifidus,* which seems to be the same, or very close to, *E. compositus.* It made a little huddle of dusty, hairy, somewhat fleshy, and many times slashed and divided small leaves about two inches high and as much across that bristle for a long period in summer with the daintiest possible pale lavender Daisies on short stems. It is quite hardy and one at least of its habitats is the Sierra Nevada at high elevations. In a rock garden it deserves a choice situation, preferably on a little sunny, stony slope with plenty of grit and humus in the soil. There it proves quite easy and at home and is certainly, in a small way, very ornamental.

With *E. flagellaris,* another small western product, I was also much intrigued, for its mats of grayish foliage sprouting lavender Daisies on five-inch stems almost throughout the summer were most engaging. But the decumbent stems rooted as they ran—and how they ran! After quickly and effectively covering their apportioned ledge they swarmed upward and downward in all directions, heedless of the shrinkings and shriekings of small hill-billies that lay in their path until *Erigeron flagellaris* bid fair to be the only sign of life that appeared in that section of the rock garden. No, this grasping little Fleabane is no plant for exclusive circles. But it is very pretty.

Erigeron mucronatus (*Vittadenia triloba*) is often offered as a good edging plant for borders, but it presents a very personable appearance also in the rock garden where, spraying this way and that over a sunny ledge, it maintains a succession of pale Daisies through the summer. This little plant is not always reliably hardy, as it comes from New Zealand and thereabouts; but it is easily raised from seed, and the seedlings bloom the first year if they have been started early in a frame or greenhouse. One has hardly begun with Erigerons; but space is limited, and there are many worthy Daisies still to be noted.

There are, for instance, the Achilleas, mostly mat-making, with gray aromatic foliage, often nicely cut, the flowers usually white, but occasionally yellow. They are easily grown in well drained sunny locations, and come readily from seed. To begin alphabetically with them: *A. ageratifolia* (*Anthemis Aizoon*) is one of the daintiest and most comely, forming a little rosette of narrow slightly woolly grayish leaves from which arise on five-inch stems pure white flowers with a yellow disc in early June. This is a really choice little plant and deserves a choice position in a sunny cleft where its roots have plenty of well drained soil to ramble in. *Achillea argentea* is another plant of real beauty, larger and more robust than the last, with masses of narrow, silvered foliage, toothed along the margins, and airy masses of pure white flowers on stems about six inches long. Like all its kind it appreciates, indeed must have, a light soil, sun and thorough drainage if it is to prove stable, but so considered it is long-lived and easy, especially if the soil is well impregnated with lime. All the Achilleas like lime.

Somewhat taller is *A. Clavennae* with mats of dull silver oval foliage and white flowers in a careless head on stems nine inches high. One might continue indefinitely with good Achilleas (as with bad); suffice it to say that worth growing are *A. Griesbachi,* from Macedonia, four inches tall and silvered as to foliage, white as to flowers; *A. Huteri,* tiny and richly aromatic, a true alpine; *A. Kelleri,* with finely divided grayish blue leaves about four inches long and heads of white flowers on nine-inch stems that are effective for a long time; *A. rupestris,* a beautiful Italian species spreading a broad mat of green, aromatic foliage and bearing large white Daisies. *A. umbellata* is much like *A. argentea* but larger throughout. It makes a delightful wall plant. This species comes from Greece. *A. tomentosa* is a yellow-flowered species, not very pretty but popular in nurseries because it is an easy doer. The leaves are woolly and pinnatifid and it grows from eight inches to a foot in height. The rather acid yellow flowers are in flat heads shaped like those of the common yarrow.

Close to Achillea is Anthemis. I will mention here only one, for *Anthemis montana* and *A. cupaniana,* as far as I can find from numerous trials, seem to be the same thing. It is a plant I have always liked to use either at the edge of a dry, sunny border or for a good-sized stretch of sunny plain in the rock garden. It makes a spreading mat of silver lace foliage, often two or three feet across, from which arise during May large, solitary, creamy Marguerites in great profusion. It is hardy and durable, but on no account will it endure the muggy damp heat to which we are too often treated in summer. I have more than once seen a whole wide platter of this valuable garden silverware melt away during a spell of extreme humidity and heat.

At least two Chrysanthemums with Daisylike flowers belong in the rock garden—*C. alpinum and C. arcticum.* The first is an alpine and not as easy to grow as one might assume from its family connections. It likes a high place in the rock garden in gritty soil and full sun. There it displays its mass of gray, deeply cut foliage and large, white, gold-eyed Daisies with nice effect in summer. The other is easily grown anywhere in the rock garden, even in partial shade, or it may be given the front place in a well drained garden border. It forms a nice bushy plant at least a foot high, its thickish leaves highly aromatic and of attractive shape. It begins to flower in late summer and continues until frost.

Asters that might, from the point of view of suitable height, be introduced into the rock garden family are many. But they should be chosen with care, for many of them spread dangerously from the root and prove but weeds among the elect. *Aster alpinus,* however, has no defects. It is a beautiful plant, easily grown, adding in its numerous varieties and forms many lovely spreads of soft color to the June display.

The Cream of the Rock Garden Daisies

The flowers are large with a conspicuous golden eye, the plant low and thrifty. A sunny situation suits it, and a soil free and not too rich. Lime chips intermingled with the soil seem to keep the plant in good shape. Numerous kinds are offered by nurseries and seed houses—*albus*, Dark Beauty, *himalaicus*, with lilac flowers and a graciously free habit of flowering, *rubra*, Goliath, and Garibaldi are all good. Once in two years the plants should be taken up, pulled to pieces, and the sections replanted.

Other desirable Asters for the rock garden are *A. Thomsoni nanus*, that used to be offered in American catalogues, but which I cannot now find; *Aster Pleiades*, a miniature Michaelmas Daisy with many lavender blossoms on branching eight-inch stems; *A. Forresti*, a very dwarf, compact sort bearing on stems four to six inches high large violet-colored flowers with a yellow disc; *A. acris nanus* makes a mat of narrow dark green leaves from which arise the leafy stems to form a little bush about ten inches high that becomes all starry with small lavender flowers in the late summer and autumn; *A. likiangensis*, a Chinese species with handsome purple flowers on stems eighteen inches high that requires a stony, not too dry soil with plenty of peat and sand; *A. Canbyi*, from the Rockies, blooming early in the summer, materializing many rosy flowers on ten-inch stems, and the eastern Bristle Aster, *A. linariifolius*, stiff, and upright to a height of some ten inches, the stems set with narrow leaves, the blossoms a nice tone of purple. This makes a fine show in September when stationed next a plantation of the common pink Heather, *Calluna vulgaris*. These two enjoy an exposed situation in rather acid soil. Good work might be done by some garden adventurer in trying out the many dwarf native Asters to find those that are safe and proper for use in the rock garden. I have often ordered a species that sounded delightful only to find that it was a violent root spreader and entirely unsafe for association with less aggressive plants. But doubtless there are many that would greatly add to our pleasure.

Arnica montana is a gay and showy plant of dwarf proportions (one foot in height) that hoists brilliant golden Daisies above a rosette of longish, soft, somewhat crumpled leaves. It is a common plant of the Alpine ranges of Europe, especially those of granite formation, but it is not easy in cultivation. Far less handsome is *A. foliosa* of our West, and far more accommodating—too accommodating, it proved here, spreading unexpectedly and untidily from the root until it had to be peremptorily put an end to. *A. montana* is the beauty of this race and will give you some deliciously bad moments getting it established.

Easier gold is to be had of Doronicum. Even the taller sorts, such as *D. caucasicum* and *D. plantagineum*, that grow eighteen inches tall and more, have the right rock garden look where there is space for them. But the real gem is a little one that blossoms very early, and which with me is seldom more than eight or ten inches tall. It came to me as *D. Clusii*, but Johnson ("Gardener's Dictionary") calls it *D. glaciale*, and Dr. Bailey ("Hortus") says it is sometimes known as *Arnica Clusii*. Both these authorities, however, disagree with the little plant as I have it. Dr. Bailey gives it much greater height, and Johnson says it flowers in July. Whatever it may be, it is a genuine find, early-flowering, bright, dwarf and compact, hardy, a first-class little plant for a low place in the rock garden and one that lasts a long time in good condition. It is said to be from Switzerland, but Correvon does not mention it.

Another good Composite for the rock garden is *Inula ensifolia,* not often seen but an attractive relative of the great Elecampane. It has the advantage of blossoming in summer when bloom in the rock garden is dim, its masses of densely leafy stems six to nine inches tall crowned by bright yellow flowers making a pleasant display in any sunny place, in any fairly good soil. On my list for trial this year from seed is another Inula, smaller by half than the last. *Inula acaulis* is described as "a quaint wee plant with huge golden flowers nestling in the leafy tufts, the whole about two inches high."

Two minute Daisies I like always to have about the rock garden in considered situations where their minuteness will show to advantage and not be put out of countenance by some bumpkin neighbor. The first is *Bellium minutum* (*B. rotundifolium*), from rocky places in Greece. It makes a flat close mat of microscopic leaves starred all over with tiny Daisies, white on the upper and lavender on the under side, through most of the summer and autumn. It is nice for an exclusive crevice in sun. The other is *Bellis rotundifolia caerulescens,* a long name for a wee beauty. It must have a sheltered and warm situation in full sun, and sometimes the parent stock will be wiped out during unusually severe weather, but the little plant takes care of this possibility by self-sowing rather freely where it is made happy. Its close mat of leaves is soft and downy and the little pale blue Marguerites are held up perkily on one-inch stems.

Coreopsis rosea, a native, may appeal to those who are trying for summer color in their rock gardens. And who is not? It will grow anywhere, though it is reported to prefer acidity and bogs. It is a spreader but if you can give it space its thickets of fine leafy stems, carrying narrow-rayed pink Daisies in great profusion, will light a corner in a modest way.

This is a most imperfect report on worth-while Daisies for the rock garden, but enough has been said to show that there are such, and that they have real value.

CHAPTER XI

THE USE OF CREEPING PLANTS IN THE
ROCK GARDEN

CREEPING plants are of great importance in clothing the rock garden with both greenery and blossoms. But it should be pointed out at once and emphatically that many of them must be used with extreme caution. The term "creeper" often underestimates their ability to get over the ground with disconcerting speed. A creeper does not stay put. Quite the contrary. It is a restless creature and advances at varying rates of speed, according to its character and how well it is suited as to soil and situation, in all directions at once, often entering the unguarded preserves of the helpless and choice little rock dwellers that sit tight and stationary, unable to protect themselves, where it smothers and strangles with relentless energy and efficiency. First know your creepers, then place them where they can do no harm, and you can then enjoy their spontaneous spread of bloom and verdure.

Certain plants which fall into the creeper class should never be allowed anywhere near a rock garden, for no matter where they are placed they arrive sooner or later where they are not wanted and proceed blithely to their work of destruction. These green destroyers are not uncommonly offered in catalogues as desirable

rock plants; but they should be avoided as the plague
by any one wishing to grow anything less hardy and
indestructible than Crab Grass or Dandelions, though
many of them have real beauty of person and grace of
port and adorn a rough bank, or a situation too trying
for grass, in a manner to be admired. Among these
outlaws are the Moneywort (*Lysimachia nummulari-
folia*), with its long green branches set with gold-piece
blossoms; the Ground Ivy (*Lamium maculatum*), of
evil odor and evil intentions; Periwinkle, of the wide
blue eyes and insatiable appetite; *Lippia repens*, a
furious ramper, though mercifully not quite hardy;
Goutweed (*Aegopodium podograria*)—and doubtless
every rock gardener could add to this blacklist out of
his own sad experience. I speak severely of Bugle-
weed, Ajuga, in public, but cherish in private several
spreads of the kind with dark shining leaves and spikes
of deep blue lipped flowers. It is catalogued as *metal-
lica crispa* and it does not display the disconcerting
activity of the ordinary *Ajuga reptans*. Besides which,
it is very handsome for carpeting a slope that would
not be given to the choicer things, and never fails in
fair weather or foul to present a seemly front.

But in the rock garden there are valleys to be clothed,
rocks to be draped, the plains where small bulbs grow
to be carpeted, the crevices between flagged paths or
stone steps to be lined with verdure; and it is in such
situations that the more conservative among the creepers come into their own. It should be here noted, however, that a plant which in one garden keeps more or
less to itself may turn out in another to be a reckless
marauder. So after all we must fall back on experience

as the best teacher, and when we find a plant taking the bit in its teeth and setting off with unconservative enthusiasm the only safe plan is to remove it summarily, and to dig over the ground to get out the smallest smitch of its roots, for these are often endowed with extraordinary vitality.

The Thymes are delightful in the creeper class; so delightful indeed, that I am saving them for a chapter all their own. Then the Linarias, the Toadflaxes. Some of these are delightful, and they do not commonly prove unmanageable in American gardens. I like very much *Linaria pallida* and its white-flowered form from Italy. They hang over stones with grace and luxuriance, little three-inch waves of greenery spangled with relatively large lilac or white sweet-scented Snapdragons, or run about freely in an open sunny situation in stony soil. They also make an uncommonly nice decoration for a flight of stone steps. The foliage dies down in winter, often a suspicious circumstance where creepers are concerned, for while activity ceases on the surface of the ground it does not by any means follow that the same is true of the roots beneath the ground, but while *Linaria pallida* is no fit companion for small Saxifrages and the like it is not a really dangerous subject in most gardens.

The Linarias take naturally to wall cultivation and the familiar Kenilworth Ivy (*L. cymbalaria*) is one often seen veiling the cool side of a wall with its pretty tracery of ivylike leaves and lilac flowers that are borne throughout the season. It seeds freely, establishing itself quickly in untenanted crevices. There is a white-flowered form that is as pretty as the type. *Linaria hepaticaefolia* is a beautiful little creeper for a half-shaded situation in the rock garden where it forms a neat and comely carpet an inch through of thickish kidney-shaped leaves prettily marked with white. It belongs to southern Europe, and the lilac blossoms are produced from June until September. The leaves are evergreen.

Another small evergreen charmer for a shaded place in wall or steps or rock garden is *L. aequitriloba*. Mr. Farrer calls this "a Tiny Tim of extraordinary charm." It grows an inch high only, and its little Toadflax blossoms are soft violet in color. It hails from Corsica. I once had a plant of *L. pilosa* that might be called a hairy edition of *L. hepaticaefolia*, but the leaves are somewhat larger and reddish on the undersides. The purple flowers are produced from June onward.

The Alpine Toadflax (*Linaria alpina*), well known and vivid, is not exactly a creeper, and in my garden does not display the persistent qualities usually attributed to it. It is, I think, a biennial, certainly not an annual, but it does not self-sow with me as it is said to do and disappears quite unaccountably. This little plant grows less than six inches in height, the leaves narrow and grayish; the flowers freely borne are of "imperial violet lipped with orange flame." Though so small, the effect of even a single plant is brilliant. A rose-colored form is said to be pretty, but I have not seen it. The Alpine Toadflax likes to be tucked into sunny crevices and endures winter damp with no grace at all. All the Linarias are easily raised from seed.

Mazus pumilio is a small but energetic New Zealander that spreads rapidly in situations not utterly parched and dry. It makes a thick, close-fitting covering for the ground, bright green and thickly studded with lilac and white gaping flowers with freckles in their throats. It is useful for the joints of steps, where it makes a flat green outline, or for little dampish valleys removed from the choice and exclusive, for it is no respecter of its betters. Sometimes a bitter winter curtails its activities, but there is always enough left to start with enthusiasm in the spring.

Lovely and choice is the dainty Corsican, *Stachys corsica*. I first grew it from seed many years ago. In a dry sunny place, preferably a little sheltered plain, in reliably drained soil, it advances circumspectly into a rolling carpet of shining green leaves above which appear all through the summer dainty small flowers of a creamy-pink tint, very pale and lovely. Whatever may be its proclivities in its own climate, the rigors of ours will never allow it to become a menace. It is one of the choicest rock garden creepers, to be cherished rather than curbed.

Among Veronicas are many attractive little rampers, some safe, some unsafe for association with the rock garden's "best." *V. rupestris* is a common beauty in most gardens, especially the bright blue-spiked kind that makes such a gay neighbor for the Maiden Pink (*Dianthus deltoides*). The two, given a wide plain and allowed their will, fight a most charming battle, mingling blue flowers with pink, and none need care very much which is the winner. The white-flowered form of *V. rupestris* is less rampant and very pretty, and *V. rupestris nana* is as circumspect a little creature as could be desired, hardly ramping at all but spreading slowly into a flat mat of green about the size of a place plate. *V. repens* holds its tiny leaves close to the earth, spreading, if happy, into wide perfectly flat mats of brightest green, veiled in spring with the palest possible shadowy blue flowers held sleekly against the green.

I have had trouble in keeping this small Corsican, not because it is especially tender, but because rude weeds thrust up through its tender expanse, and in getting them out the plant is invariably badly injured, sometimes unto death. A flat ledge in light soil is a good place for it and weeds should be eradicated while they are very small. I find it suffers in spells of extreme drought, so it should not be allowed to go unwatered. It is the carpet of all others for the smallest and choicest of bulbous things. *V. armena* is wholly delightful, and seemingly little known. It makes mounds of lax branches five inches long, clothed like little fir branches in soft narrow leaves out of which appear in May airy sprays of bright blue flowers. The best companion for it on a little plain is *Androsace sarmentosa,* or one of its close kin, for when they mingle their blue sprays and their pink umbrellas they present a gay spectacle indeed.

V. nummularia is another species that is not well known, but worth growing. It is circumspection itself, making a neat little mat of inch-tall stems clothed in evergreen leaves above which the bright blue flowers show prettily in June. It is for lightly shaded situations in gritty soil in which some humus has been mixed.

Other personable Veronicas in the creeper class are *V. pectinata* and its rose-colored form, with gray foliage, blossoming in June, that requires a well-drained situation in sun and protection from the attentions of stronger plants; *V. saxatilis,* both blue-flowered and white, that makes evergreen mats scarcely an inch high, that will never give trouble to their neighbors; and of course there is *V. filiformis,* that one hardly dares mention in a complimentary way, so disconcertingly speedy is it in getting over the ground, so greedy in appropriating space that is allotted to other plants. Yet it is lovely with its lush two-inch masses of leaves on thread-fine stems and the cloud of blue and white blossoms that in April and May sweeps over it. Nothing more innocent-appearing could be found in the world of flowers. But it should have a bank all to itself far from temptation. Small plants are not safe in its vicinity. It gobbles them up in less time, almost, than it takes to tell about it and then flows as smoothly as a placid green river above their little drowned bodies.

Arenaria balearica spreads bright green and moss-like in a cool position, sheeting stones and ground alike with smooth green verdure that is swept in season by a milky way of white stars. English writers warn of its "minute but undivorceable embrace," but our drought-ridden climate and burning suns keep it in check. To keep it with us at all is the difficult thing.

Numerous Androsaces are in the creeper class, chief among them *A. sarmentosa* and its variety *Chumbyi,* that raise fetching pink umbrellas above spreads of gray silky rosettes, and *A. lanuginosa* with long trailing shoots set with silver leaves, above which arise in May, and off and on through the summer and autumn, Verbenalike heads of blush-colored blossoms. Any sandy, sunny plain or slope on the rock garden will do for these, but they should be top-dressed in spring and in autumn with a mixture of sand and humus if the wide mats are to be kept in good condition.

Antennaria dioica rosea is also a good carpeter, flat and neat and silvery, but far-reaching if given its head. In summer it sprouts little two-inch stems of pinkish everlasting flowers, not as pretty as the foliage. It will grow anywhere and is not for a choice position, though very pretty in appearance, spreading smoothly down a little hillside or lining a small valley with its silver satin verdure.

A beautiful carpeter for an exposed situation, high and wind-swept, is *Dryas octopetala.* This little shrub makes wide sheets of small Oaklike leaves and bears in late spring and summer large creamy blossoms filled with golden stamens that put one in mind of little single Roses. It grows most freely where the soil is impregnated with lime, and is one of the finest of rock plants. It requires a yearly top-dressing with sand and humus.

Last year for the first time *Convolvulus mauritanicus* bloomed in my garden. I had seen it in England and Scotland making generous spreads of hairy leaves almost obliterated by the crowding Morning Glories of clearest lilac-blue. I thought it one of the most lovely things I had ever seen, but understood it to be a southerner that would not stand our climate. However, a plant was secured, and the breathless succession of blossoms enjoyed all summer. In the autumn I said farewell to it, grateful for having had it for the single season. What was my surprise and delight this spring to find it briskly sprouting anew, and that after our winter of most unusual cold. It is growing on a ledge in the rock garden facing south, with a rock at its back to keep off the north winds; the soil is light and well drained, and it received the same light covering of salt hay that was given the rest of the garden. And it lived through. This is one of those surprises that give the rock gardener a distinct thrill. No one should miss *Convolvulus mauritanicus*. My plant came from a nursery in the Northwest, and not expecting it to live I had ordered two more for this spring, so now I shall have a wealth of blueness indeed. *C. incanus*, that Mr. Farrer calls a gem of ray serene, I am obliged to characterize as a dangerous nuisance, once it is established, and nothing is easier than to establish it. It is an American plant and makes little low tufts of velvet leaves out of which appear blush-colored Morning Glories, all very low and neat and tufty. So far, so good. But it is an indefatigable underground spreader, advancing its velvet tufts with feverish speed, and not to be got rid of by wishing or even by sterner means. I shall always have it perforce, but I should never suffer it if I could live my life over again.

Gypsophila cerastioides is a neat creeper that comes from the mid-alpine regions of Kashmir and Sikkim. It is prettier and less straggling, as well as less frequently grown than *G. repens*, which trails bountifully over a rock face in full sun. *G. cerastioides* is low and compact, yet advances sufficiently to be described as a creeper. Its leaves are hairy and thickish, and the large white flowers are of good substance and prettily veined with purple. I've not found this plant among the easiest to keep happy. It has a way of going off in a huff and giving one no notion of what it found distasteful. I rather think it is the heavy humidity of our summers, for it always starts the spring with a certain amount of zest, seeming to lose heart as the summer advances.

Hypericum reptans stands out among its golden-flowered family as one of the most precious. It covers the ground with amazing vigor, holding its small-leaved greenery close to the earth and all during the summer spattering it with great yellow stars, red-brown in the bud. This beautiful plant should have a prominent situation, a rocky promontory over which it can creep and trail and show off its points. Yet it wants some shelter, too. My plant faces west and is protected on the north by a high rock with a Yew behind it. It has been contented for a number of years, and ever widens the sphere of its charming activity.

There are a number of creeping Phloxes, among them *P. stolonifera,* with heads of rose-colored flowers on stems four inches high. It spreads by means of runners and rooting stolons and, given a good stretch of ground, will quickly overlay it with its tender branches and oval leaves. I have a lavender-flowered form that seems to be close to it but is prettier and has the added charm of delicious fragrance. *P. stolonifera* is a native of the more southerly eastern states—Kentucky, southern Pennsylvania, and Georgia. With me it never becomes a nuisance.

There are of course many other creepers—including Cerastium, Saponaria, Sedums, *Euphorbia Myrsinites,* and Acaenas—but these are quite a handful to carry on with.

CHAPTER XII

NATURE would seem to have been in one of her kindliest and most gracious moods when she created the Thymes. They are of the earth's most fragrant and pleasant greenery. To collect the different kinds, to work among them, to know them well are richly rewarded pursuits that any one with a patch of earth of whatever size should be able to follow, for they require little care and multiply generously, asking only sunshine and a well drained soil. But it is not, after all, such easy going—not a mere reaching out and taking, or offering a small sum in exchange for a little scented bushling or mat of aromatic green. At least not in this country where our horticultural eagerness is so sharply curbed by Quarantine 37. No Thyme is indigenous to the United States, nor indeed to the American continents, though the Creeping Thyme, *Thymus Serpyllum*, is to be found prowling about old fields and along roadsides in long settled neighborhoods from Nova Scotia to New York and Pennsylvania, having escaped from gardens to this freedom. However, a lucky wayfarer may sometimes chance upon a bank where the wild Thyme blows, or some windy upland where the little creeper has made free with a meadow as it does in its native lands.

[99]

But to make a comprehensive collection of Thymes means turning the pages of many American catalogues, gleaning one kind here, one kind there, comparing one to another, matching them up with reliable descriptions to be sure we have what we hope we have and being disappointed that the number of kinds available is so limited. Then turning to seed catalogues, domestic and foreign, making lists and dispatching them, raising the little plants from seed and again matching and comparing to be sure we have what we hope we have. Knowing extreme disappointment sometimes, again keen jubilation.

All this chanciness and uncertainty doubtless adds to the zest the collector feels, keeps him in a healthy state of curiosity and activity. But it would be nice to be able to lay by the heels some of the recently introduced little rarities with somewhat less effort and travail. However, as any gardener knows, the seemingly beyond-his-reach may come to him any day by some means or other if he wishes hard enough, for wishes often are in very truth father to plants.

Chiefly the Thymes belong to the hills of the countries bordering the Mediterranean, to the islands in this blue sea, to central Asia, and one or two, I believe, to Russia and North Africa. All that I have been able to lay hands upon have proved hardy in my garden in the neighborhood of New York, and I have news of their hardiness in much severer climates, especially where the snow lies deep and long during the winter. But they must be given sunny situations and a free gritty soil. Their uses are many and invariably sweet. There are two types, creepers and erect forms, with

some that come in between, that are neither quite prostrate nor yet quite erect, but shrubby and low and
spready. The bushling types are obviously valuable
for use as low shrubbery in the rock garden and appear
well planted in the chinks of a sunny wall face. In the
rock garden the creeping Thymes transform the harsh
outlines of stones and boulders into softly padded hum-
mocks. Planted between the stones of paths and steps,
they create rivers of flowing fragrant green or gray.

Especial care should be taken not to allow weeds to
settle themselves among the creeping Thymes. Such
conscienceless invaders as the little yellow-flowered
Oxalis, Chickweed, or the fast traveling white Clover
can so insinuate their rootlets among those of the trust-
ing Thyme that to eradicate them will completely de-
stroy the fine green carpet, yet to let them remain would
also mean speedy destruction. The only sure way is to
watch the Thyme carpets well and to extract any alien
growths before they have had a chance to get started
on their career of depredation. The Thyme mats are
well worth preserving in their integrity, for not only
are their flower-powdered surfaces a delight to look
upon in the summer months when they bloom, but the
soft carpets are a pleasure to sit or walk upon, enduring such usage with complacency and giving us a greeting of fragrance that is second to none known to me
for sweetness.

The leafage of the Thymes is small, usually close-
set, dusty gray or green, and the little lipped blossoms,
not conspicuous save for their generous numbers, come
in tones of mauve and rose to carmine and white.

Once every self-respecting garden patch grew the

common kitchen Thyme, *Thymus vulgaris,* used for seasoning; today we buy it in a package and so this pleasant little shrub, some six inches high with dusty-looking evergreen leaves and woody stems, and a powdering of pale flowers, is absent from most gardens, though it is easily grown from seed and to be had of any seedsman in one or another of its forms. There is the English broad-leaved kind, also French and German products, much resembling each other; but one form I have, which came to me a few years ago, stands out from among them because of its especially delicious fragrance—as sweet as, and much resembling, Rose Geranium. This is known as *Thymus fragrantissimus,* and it is said to have been found by an English seedsman in a cottage garden. On a height in my rock garden it makes a huddle of little gray bushes, spready and twiggy, and self-sows freely, the little Fir-like progeny coming up all about and proving very useful where other things have failed. We dry the branches for seasoning.

The Creeping Thyme, *Thymus Serpyllum,* known also as Mother of Thyme, Hillwort, Pella Mountain, Shepherd's Thyme, and so on, in its many forms spreads seductive traceries far and wide in the rock garden and between the stones of paths and walls. These are among the most valuable of carpeting plants, delightful in or out of bloom. The small blossoms literally blot out the green mat in early summer and last a long time. Two very bright-hued kinds are *Th. S. coccineus* and *Th. S. splendens,* but the loveliest and most desirable to my mind is the white-flowered Thyme, *Th. S. albus.* The leaves are minute, but it spreads into yard-wide mats in the rock garden; and its pale flowering is like a Milky Way come to earth. However far it may roam, I never have the heart to curb its wanderings. A form with flesh-pink flowers known as *Th. S. carneus,* and said to be very lovely, I have not yet seen.

Familiar to most gardeners is the so-called Woolly Thyme, *Th. S. lanuginosus.* With me its pale blooms are very charily produced; but its silvery, soft foliage is somehow flowerlike in appearance, and wide mats of it are always effective flowing among the stones in the rock garden or spreading down a sunny wall face. The Woolly Thyme is one of the very best plants to use as a carpet above small choice bulbs, providing at once a becoming setting for their delicate beauty and preserving it from defacement by mud spattered up by the wild spring storms. It can be a danger to small choice plants if not watched, for all it looks so innocent; but it is valuable in the right place, as is another woolly form, *Th. villosus,* which I have not yet found in this country.

There are numerous other forms of the Creeping Thyme that you may chance upon in your search— *Th. S. aureus,* the foliage of which turns "golden" in winter; *Th. S. nummularius,* that I have not found in the flesh, but which I have in the frames for spring germination (I hope); *Th. S. Marshalli,* and others— all having a general resemblance one to another, save the woolly forms that are quite distinct. *Thymus azoricus,* from the Azores, is also a creeper, absolutely prostrate as I have it, with dark foliage that covers itself with a purple scarf in midsummer and has to my nose something of the fragrance of Tangerines.

This may be just another form of the creeping Thyme.

By some authorities the Lemon Thyme, *Th. citriodorus,* is given as a form of *Serpyllum* but it is so distinct in appearance as to seem to deserve a separate identity. It makes a woody, spreading, low, wiry-stemmed bush, not a creeper, though it forms broad masses. The leaves of the type are green and somewhat shining and smell deliciously of lemons and some sort of spice. I find the Lemon Thyme is occasionally injured not by winter weather but by the searing spring winds, after the covering has been removed in early spring. I have had to learn to leave a light covering of salt hay on these plants rather longer than on the rest of the garden. The Lemon Thyme has two very decorative forms, one a very old garden favorite known to Parkinson as the Embroidered or Gilded Thyme "that smelleth of Pomecitron." This is *Th. citriodorus aureus* to us, and has leaves edged with yellow. Then there is the Silver-Leaved Thyme, *Th. c. argenteus,* with leaves distinctly marked with "silver." Both these are very valuable in the rock garden and grace with distinction a little promontory or cliff where the matted branches can spill over the sides. Silver Queen is a greatly improved form of *argenteus* that I have not yet found in this country, but which I saw in England used effectively in many rock gardens.

A few years ago I was much pleased to find in this country a Thyme that was wholly new to me, and that had very definite and different charms of fragrance. This is *Th. herba-barona* and it comes from the sunny hills of the island of Corsica. I have been surprised to see it described in some English catalogues as erect-growing. The form I have is quite prostrate and the odor it gives forth when brushed is strongly that of Caraway. How different and misleading, however, is the testimony of noses! Jason Hill, that exact observer and delightful writer, most surprisingly describes the fragrance of *herba-barona* as resembling that of Sassafras! I was, so to speak, brought up on Sassafras—one of youth's most favored nibbling leaves—and I do not think this Thyme has any resemblance to it. However, it was a most gratifying find, and my grief was poignant when during a wet and muggy spell my one plant melted away and died. When replaced it was given a sunnier exposure on a steep and well-drained slope where it has since thriven through an abnormally wet and humid summer and an abnormally cold winter, so I take it that it has settled down in comfort. But I have not yet seen the little purple rondels of bloom to which it is said to give birth.

Last year *Thymus Zygis* arrived in my garden through the generosity of Helen Fox, who had raised it from seed. It is the neatest possible little procumbent shrublet, no more than three inches high and a good deal broader, very stiff and twiggy, with oblong linear leaves of a nice scent. The Kew Hand-List reports it as native of Spain and Portugal. In Mrs. Fox's garden it grew in a sunny wall face. The flowers are said to be pink.

Thymus membranaceus is an especially desirable and scarce species. It was introduced recently from the Sierra Nevada in Spain. I lost the tiny shoot of it I received from a central western nurseryman through not giving this baby mountaineer sufficient care and shall mourn it until it is replaced. It is described as "a dense greyish green, sweetly scented cushion with large, upstanding, cone-shaped heads of tightly packed whitish pink flushed bracts with the delicate tubular flowers coming out between." Any lover of alpine flowers must be enchanted at its appearance and covet it at once. To have lost it is a real tragedy; to find it again is my constant hope.

Among the erect-growing kinds should be mentioned *Th. nitidus,* sometimes described as resembling a miniature Irish Yew, silvery gray and covering itself in early summer with rosy lilac flowers. It grows nine inches high and as much through, and the whole plant is very sweetly scented. Seed of it is to be had and also of *Th. erectus,* growing a foot tall and looking like a little tree. *Th. carnosus,* an upright-growing sort I have not yet been able to find—either seeds or plants—nor have I discovered *Th. Doerfleri,* introduced by Mr. Ingwersen from the Balkans, said to be one inch high, "neatly grey leaved and mat forming and covered with rich red, sweet scented flowers." All these sound desirable, and I am on the watch for them.

CHAPTER XIII

DECIDUOUS and evergreen shrubs play the same vital and significant part in the rock garden that they do in any part of the grounds or in the natural landscape. They should properly be of diminutive size but otherwise the types and the rôles they are called to assume are identical. Of course the size of the rock garden and its scale will determine the height and spread of the shrubs admitted, and there is always place in its environs, its setting, for somewhat larger specimens, even for small trees. But here we are concerned chiefly with the genuinely dwarf woody plants. And when we have decided this our troubles have only just begun, for little shrubs are extremely scarce in this country. With infinite pains and no little fasting (literally) I have assembled my small collection, and were it not for the natives among them it would be even more meager than it is in comparison with the wealth available to gardeners in other parts of the world.

Many of the small shrubs are possessed of great charm. They display all the variety of mien and deportment shown by their prototypes of greater stature, and none of the unpleasant freakishness of dwarfs of the human race. Some are slender and willowy, some upright and stiff, some low and crouching, others quite

[107]

prostrate. Whatever the situation to be filled, whether a height emphasized, a gorge filled with tangled underbrush, a cliff to be masked, there is a little shrub to do the work, if only we can find it, and it is only by means of these small woody plants that we may endow our mountain landscape with realism. In winter the evergreens, broad-leaved and narrow-leaved, give life to the scenery; in summer they lend it stability and richness, while the deciduous kinds are interesting all the year through because of their varied forms and habits and the hues of their foliage and branches.

Spiraeas

The small Spiraeas are effective and neat. The first I had was *S. crispifolia* (*S. bullata*), a quaint little Japanese, stocky and erect to a height of about a foot, with dark crinkled leaves and heads of pinkish crimson small flowers finishing each branch in the late summer. It has lived in my garden for more than ten years and seems quite hardy, increasing its girth with circumspection.

Then came *Spiraea decumbens*, a delightful small thing a few inches high and much in the slender style of the Bridal Wreath, which Mr. Farrer says runs freely about among the sunny stony places of the limestone screes of the Dolomites "with little arching shoots set delicately with small well-proportioned toothed grey leaves and bearing loose galaxies of milk-pure stars throughout the summer on bending sprays of four or five inches, half flopping and half standing, but always of incomparable charm and sweetness of aspect." It is very delightful to possess this small beauty and to know that it will gradually spread into a thicket a foot across. It is in the newly constructed moraine and seems very happy there. *Spiraea caespitosa* (*Petrophytum caespitosum*) is an American and comes from limestone regions in Montana, South Dakota, and California. It is quite distinct in appearance, forming thick carpets of narrow silvery evergreen leaves from which arise during most of the summer midget spikes of fluffy white flowers no more than three inches high. This also is a plant that likes the moraine though probably any well drained, stony place would do as well. With these I have another that I am unable to identify— *Spiraea Hendersoni*. I received it this spring from a nursery in the Northwest, and it is very quaint and attractive in appearance. Its sponsor says it makes small mounds or domes four to six inches high, the foliage turning to a bronzy red in fall and winter. Small heads of fluffy white or pinkish flowers all summer. A treasure, it sounds to me. I received it from William Borsch of Maplewood, Oregon.

The Little Willows

There are numerous small Willows that fit nicely the contours of the rock garden, and some slightly taller ones that may well be used in its setting. They are not showy, but they are amusing; they bear quaint catkins in spring, and certain of them are quite prostrate, clinging to the ground as to a last hope, or fitting snugly over a rock. *Salix retusa* lived in my garden for ten years or more. Then a neighbor's dog elected to bury his bone beneath it. It was clawed up and finished off then and there. Poor little faithful Willow! It is a quite prostrate species from the mountains of Europe, with glabrous branches that root firmly to the ground as they travel, making dense carpets of lustrous small leaves and displaying the characteristic jolly catkins in spring. There is a smaller-leaved variety named *serpyllifolia,* but I have not come across it. *Salix reticulata* is somewhat less desirable, though withal attractive, low, and procumbent, slightly downy. It is a native of North America from Labrador to Alaska, as well as of Europe and northern Asia.

Salix brachycarpa is a small American Willow whose height does not exceed one foot. It has yellow twigs and branches and is all complete with funny little catkins. It grows naturally from British Columbia and Washington to Colorado and Utah. Not many good things native in his part of the world escape the eye of D. M. Andrews of Boulder, Colorado, so it is not surprising that this small Willow should appear in his catalogue. He lists another that I do not yet know—*S. saximontana,* "the most diminutive species, only an inch in height, forming small mats." This sounds very desirable. Years ago I had from him *S. glaucops* that grows two feet high, is decked with silvery leaves and makes the most enchanting Lilliput display of catkins in spring. There are numerous other small Willows. A field is here for investigation, but it should be by one who cares for the quieter things. One who wants a splash will not care for the little Willows.

The Little Brooms

These comprise a most important part of the rock garden's shrub outfit. They are deciduous, of various heights, from absolutely prostrate to those attaining many feet, and they bear pea-shaped flowers in yellow, white, or pink; for the most part they are yellow. Under the banner of the rock garden Brooms ride certain species of Cytisus, Genista, and, I had hoped, Ulex, in its dwarf form *nanus*. But this dainty little Gorse, though easily raised from seed, has not proved hardy with me.

Genista and Cytisus are close to each other and cataloguists mix them badly. I do not know, however, that it greatly matters so we acquire them under one name or the other. They all want warm, well drained situations in gritty soil and sunshine. All the very small ones that I have tried have come through the severest weather safely; some of the taller ones have proved less hardy, being cut badly and in a few cases killed outright. To begin with Cytisus: *C. Ardoinii* is a minute prostrate sprawling plant that comes from the heights above the Mediterranean. In late April it is alight with surprisingly large and very bright yellow flowers. It deserves a choice nook and a hot rock to creep over. *C. Ardoinii* and *C. Beanii*—the latter a little bush with yellow flowers—are the parents of a most charming sort named *C. kewensis*. This has creamy fragrant flowers and branches that will shower down a rock face most effectively. *C. leucanthus* (*C. schipkaensis*) I raised from seed and so far know only as a little gray-green bush that, however, looks very promising. If it lives up to specifications, it will be low and spready and in season covered with creamy flowers. *C. purpureus* is a nice semi-upright bush for high sunny places. It ultimately grows eighteen inches tall and in May bears pinkish or purplish flowers in some profusion. *C. de-*

What Happens in My Garden

cumbens (*Genista prostrata*) spreads wiry branches widely over a sunny rock and in May strings them with characteristic pea-shaped yellow blossoms.

Of Genistas the most wholly fascinating is *G. dalmatica,* a low furzy little shrub spreading deliberately to the size of a dinner plate and rising to a height of only three or four inches. In May its entire prickly surface is obscured beneath a cloud of golden bloom. Lovely for a little cliff where it may hang in the sun. *G. radiata* is an amusing spidery little bushlet about a foot tall and as much through. *G. sagittalis* is a curious but showy species with sprawling winged branches that produce innumerable spikes of brilliant yellow flowers in early summer. It wants a hot plain to spread over and a lean soil for diet.

There are numerous other somewhat taller forms of both Genista and Cytisus if you have space for them. *Genista hispanica* makes a round gold-flowered bush two feet high, and the double form of the Dyer's Green-weed, *G. tinctoria fl. pl.* is showy for an unwanted corner. The lovely white Spanish Broom, and the many fine forms of the Common Broom, *Cytisus scoparius,* as well as *C. nigricans* are fine background material, or may be used on the heights of really spacious rock gardens.

Rock Garden Roses

Even to the rock garden the queen of flowers sends her representatives. The little Roses are of a special fascination. Quaint and beguiling and minute is a newcomer—*Rosa Rouletti.* This was found some years ago in a Swiss mountain village—or so the story goes— by a Colonel Roulet, growing on the window ledges of the cottages. Colonel Roulet reported his find to his friend Henri Correvon, and the two set forth to capture this treasure. When they arrived at the village they found it had been destroyed by fire the night before. Not a little Rose was to be found. However, the gods that smile upon gardeners (at times) smiled this time, and a single plant was found in a neighboring village. From this small foundling the stock that today brightens our rock gardens was developed. No more enchanting small shrub could be found. It grows but three or four inches tall; its leaves are small, its habit compact, its buds tiny, and its pink blooms the size of a dime. They are borne off and on all through the summer. It should be given a sunny situation in good well-drained soil, well out of the damp. So it proves hardy.

Rosa foliolosa alba, the Texas Rose, grows perhaps ten inches high, is nicely bushy, and bears all summer a procession of inch-wide creamy, fragrant flowers. It is perfectly hardy and neatly ornamental. Dr. Burlingham, one of our most accomplished rock gardeners, in an article in the short-lived *New York Gardens,* speaks also of *Rosa Lyonii,* which, he says, is much like the foregoing save for an inch more height and the fact that the blossoms are clear pink in color. This too is a native wild Rose, found from Massachusetts to Minnesota, south and west. Dr. Burlingham speaks of how charming they are grown together, and of the delightful effect in autumn of their reddish stems and multicolored leaves.

Rosa alpina I have bought and paid for but never received. However, a pretty double-flowered and very generous little plant is here masquerading for it. The blooms are blush-colored when they should be deep crimson. Carl Purdy lists a tiny Rose that he says grows only two or three inches high, which spreads by means of underground roots into wide colonies. It is *R. spithamea,* said to be found from Oregon into California. It sounds alluring. Mention is made in the chapter on Roses of *R. nitida* and *R. arkansana;* both are suitable for use in the rock garden, and doubtless many more could be added from our rich store of wild Roses by one setting out to collect them seriously.

Daphnes

Of the numerous and very lovely Daphnes suitable for our use very few are available thus far in this country. Curiously enough *D. Cneorum,* though not an easily grown plant, is the only one commonly found in our nurseries. It is, however, highly desirable and lovely, and any pains we expend in an effort to placate it are worth while, though it must be confessed as often as not wasted. It is strange that such a naughty plant should be so popular. Its lax evergreen branches, each finished by a flat head of waxen heavenly sweet pink flowers, are to be seen in various stages of sickness and health in every premeditated rock pile throughout the country. And it is not always those who have gone to the most trouble in its behalf that are the most richly rewarded. I believe, after many trials and failures and a little final success, that the secret lies in a deep soil made up of leaf mold, loam, and plenty of limestone chips, or a naturally limy soil. There is a lovely white-flowered form offered across the border.

Daphne Blagayana from the eastern Alps is also in

my garden, doing very well. It came through the past bitter winter without losing a branch and with only a light covering of salt hay to protect it from the wintry blasts. In early April each leafy branch was finished with a cluster of exquisitely fragrant creamy white flowers. Its situation is on a south-facing slope, but it receives some shade on the west from a distant tree. Its soil is very stony and well drained.

My single bush of *Daphne Genkwa* has for me a special significance and value, for it once grew in the garden of my old friend the late Clarence Lown, of Poughkeepsie. It is a weakly little bush about two and a half feet high, irregular and seemingly irresolute. Each year I think it has perished, so long do its dark branches remain impassive. And then one day in May I find it has thought better of its sulks and hung itself most surprisingly with sweet lavender-pink flowers that are quickly followed by the leaves. It requires a sheltered place and, I think, much tender care.

D. alpina is the latest of the race to reach my garden. I know little about it yet save that it came through last winter safely. It should grow into a low bushlet, "twisted and branching, no more than a foot or eighteen inches high." In spring a few heads of milk-white, scented stars unfold and the oval blue-gray leaves appear. Like all Daphnes this one is said to have a weakness for lime. All the race, too, resent disturbance. If they must be moved as large a ball of earth as possible should go with them and we must be patient until they have recovered from the shock. Where may we find in this country *D. petraea, D. Collina,* and the many other desirable dwarf species?

What Happens in My Garden

Heathers

Callunas and Ericas play important rôles in the furnishing of the rock garden. *Calluna vulgaris* is a small evergreen shrub with nodding flowers in terminal spikes in the late summer. It ranges in color in the different horticultural forms, of which there are many, from white to deep crimson and purple. A collection of Callunas in an appropriate situation is an attractive feature in any rock garden. Every year they should be cut over lightly after flowering to keep them compact and shapely. Now and again a hard winter will prune them but they are seldom killed outright in this locality if the soil they grow in is light and well drained. Some good forms are *Alportii*, carmine; *Hammondii*, white; *coccinea*, very bright; *aurea*, dwarf and compact with thick golden foliage; *Foxii*, dwarf and matted; *nana*, only four inches high.

The Ericas are charming evergreen shrubs with minute foliage and bell-shaped flowers. There is a vast number of species, some very tall, but those that have proved hardy and satisfactory here in the rock garden are the following: *E. carnea* is less than a foot tall. It blossoms so early in the year that I have often drawn the little bloom-encrusted branches from beneath the snow. There are numerous horticultural forms of it, some very bright in color and all desirable. *E. ciliaris*, Fringed Heath, grows a foot tall and has rosy flowers in terminal racemes in the late summer. *E. cinerea*, Twisted Heath, grows a little taller and bears its rosy flowers almost throughout the summer. *E. Tetralix* has larger bells than the others, rose-colored,

[116]

and the leaves are whitish on the undersides. An effective sort. *E. vagans,* Cornish Heath, grows somewhat less than a foot tall and bears in leafy racemes pretty purplish pink bells. There are a white and a deeper pink sort. These are all profuse bloomers and seem to like a sandy, peaty soil in sun. They should be grown in masses if they are to be appreciated for what they are worth.

Heathlike Plants

Andromeda polifolia. Evergreen with creeping rootstock and upright usually little branched stems. Oblong to linear leaves and white or pink flowers in April. Newfoundland and Labrador and south to New Jersey. Damp places. Very hardy.

Arctostaphylos Uva-ursi. Bearberry. Prostrate, creeping, evergreen shrub, with shining leaves, natural to pine barrens in various parts of the United States. Makes wide patches, and in spring matures small globe-shaped white flowers amidst the shining foliage.

Bruckenthalia spiculifolia. Spike Heath. A little Ling from Asia Minor and southeastern Europe, with slender upright branches and tiny leaves. Mr. Farrer refers to it as sheeting the mountains of Bulgaria in its mats of close brilliant green fur. It is hardy here in a bed of sandy peat but has been shy about showing its small pink flowers.

Chiogenes hispidula. Creeping Snowberry. Attractive creeping evergreen woody plants for a cool shaded place in the rock garden. The almost threadlike stems spread lovingly over the earth and are set with tiny oval leaves that turn rusty in autumn. Its flowers are small white bells, but with me it has not matured the little white berries that should follow. Native of high mountains of eastern North America.

Diapensia lapponica. I have failed to satisfy this lovely little fairylike plant. It is a very low tufted evergreen and should bear many small white bell-shaped blooms. It is from our highest eastern mountains.

Epigaea repens. Trailing Arbutus. Mayflower. Now that we may buy this exquisitely fragrant flower of the spring in pots, we are more likely to succeed with it. It seems to prefer acid soil in sun or half-shade. After planting, it is well to keep it mulched with leaves for a season until it has become established.

Gaultheria procumbens. Wintergreen. Checkerberry. A little creeping evergreen plant with shining leaves and white flowers followed by scarlet berries.

Gaylussacia brachycera. Box Huckleberry. A quaint little Huckleberry found growing in dry woods and sandy barrens in the eastern states. It grows only a few inches high, has creeping stems and white or pink bells in May. Acid soil in sun or shade.

Leiophyllum buxifolium. Sand Myrtle. A neat evergreen shrub growing about eighteen inches tall with small shining leaves, and in spring covered with white or pinkish flowers. There is a prostrate form known as *L. Lyoni,* or *L. prostratum,* that is very desirable for small rock gardens. The first is native of sandy barrens from New Jersey to Florida, the other is found in the mountains of North Carolina and Tennessee. Sun and a sandy peaty soil.

Shrubs for the Rock Garden

Vaccinium Vitis-idaea. Cowberry. A little shrub with evergreen leaves that turn bronze in the autumn, and white or pink flowers in short nodding racemes in early summer. Europe and northern Asia. There is a prostrate, creeping form found in high places from Alaska to Massachusetts. This is known as var. *minus,* the Creeping Cowberry.

Small Rhododendrons

There are a great many of these listed in foreign catalogues and garden books, but they are few and expensive in this country. They like shade and a lime-free soil, and are not otherwise difficult to deal with. The famous Rose des Alpes, *R. ferrugineum,* a small specimen, was secured after years of search. It has dark shining leaves, rusty beneath, and small pink to carmine flowers in June. *R. racemosum* is neat and amazingly floriferous, even when only a few inches tall. The little shoots are sometimes clothed almost their whole length with pretty blush-colored flowers. It is easy and hardy. The small Rhododendrons like plenty of broken stone in their soil to help conserve moisture for their fine thirsty roots. A mulch of leaves in our dry summers is an appreciated consideration. *R. canadense* (*Rhodora canadensis*), a native plant from northern bogs, is delightful for damp places. It covers its leaf-less branches in early spring with purple butterfly-like blooms. The tiny Alpine Azalea, *Loiseleuria procumbens,* from our White Mountains is also here in a small guarded specimen. It is quite prostrate and, I hope, will some day bear for me its small white or rose flowers.

Other Small Shrubs

A further list of small shrubs suitable for use in a rock garden would include *Abelia chinensis;* numerous Artemisias; *Berberis buxifolia, B. verruculosa,* both evergreen; several small Cotoneasters, including *C. humifusa; Ceanothus americanus; Dryas octopetala; Empetrum nigrum;* dwarf Lavender; Micromerias; *Muehlenbeckia nana,* quite prostrate; *Pachistima Canbyi; Potentilla fruticosa;* Santolina; Satureia, and *Teucrium Marum,* a little sweet-scented shrub from Mediterranean regions.

Conifers

These must be searched for with the proverbial fine-toothed comb in the great mass of tall-growing species and varieties that clutter our nurseries. Naturally dwarf-growing Conifers are hard to come by, and one reads with an envious heart the lists in European catalogues. The following may be looked for with some hope of success: *Abies balsamea hudsonia; Chamaecyparis obtusa nana* and several other genuinely dwarf forms; *Juniperus communis depressa, J. Sabina; Picea glauca albertiana, P. excelsa nana, P. e. Gregoryana, P. e. Maxwellii, P. e. pygmaea* (these five are of the utmost importance and usefulness); *Pinus montana* (Mugo); *Taxas canadensis,* and some of the spreading Japanese forms for spacious rock gardens.

CHAPTER XIV

THE GLAMOROUS SILENES

IN ALL the recipes for happiness I have ever seen, "something to look forward to" has been given as an important ingredient. Something to look forward to! How rich the gardener, any gardener, is in this particular integrant! For always he looks forward to something if it is only the appearance of the red noses of the Peonies in spring or the sharp aroma that fills the air in autumn after the frost has touched the herbage. My cold frames especially give me something to look forward to. They are divided into neat squares, each square with a label in the center about which is sown the seed of some plant usually new to me. There are a hundred and fifty such squares, all containing something that fires my imagination and fills me with anticipation. Among them this year are several Silenes I have not before grown; one is *S. flavescens,* presumably with yellow flowers, and the idea of a yellow-flowered Silene in this pink and white and scarlet family intrigues me mightily.

Growing Silenes has proved a most beguiling enterprise despite the fact that Reginald Farrer pronounces them "a race of low general attractiveness." After this pronouncement, however, he lingers over some of them with obvious delight and many complimentary adjec-

tives. It was his alluring descriptions of his favorites
that long ago incited me to extend my knowledge of
the family beyond the pretty little biennial *S. pendula,*
so pink and useful for edging beds and borders, and
Lobel's Catchfly, a pretty old-fashioned annual plant
growing a foot tall and bearing heads of bright rose-
purple flowers on sticky stems. Then I met with *S. pennsylvanica,* tufting the hills of Westchester County,
and my interest in the race became acute. No one
could accuse this lovely flower of low general attractiveness.

The genus Silene, known familiarly as Catchfly and
Campion, is a member of the Pink family—Caryophyl-
laceae. Authority states their number as being some
four or five hundred scattered over North and South
America, North Africa, and temperate Asia. Many of
them may in fact be nondescript and of small account,
but to an outstanding few the word "glamour" is not
excessive; there is about them a magic enchantment, a
delusive or alluring beauty or charm, which is the defi-
nition given by the dictionary of the overworked word.

It is not claiming too much, I think, to state that
the most beautiful of the Silenes belong to North
America, and it is also safe to say that they are far
better known abroad than in their own country, which
is a matter for us to feel ashamed of. There is, for
instance, the before-mentioned *S. pennsylvanica,* called
the American Wild Pink, or by "Standardized Plant
Names" most uneuphoniously "Peatpink." This plant
has the appearance of a choice alpine, yet it is a lovely
"common" gypsy roving the rocky hills from eastern
Massachusetts to New York, Kentucky, and the South-

west. It is a low tufted plant blooming explosively in spring, its pure pink notched blossoms making a brilliant display for several weeks. Pale and deep forms are found, but always the color is pure and untouched by any magenta stain; I have heard of, but have never seen, an albino.

Mr. Durand in his writings about wild flowers urges that this plant be purchased rather than dug from the wild, for it is in danger of extinction; but where it may be rescued from the march of that Juggernaut, the development scheme, it is an act of pure mercy to remove it to safety. But let the would-be rescuer remember that the root is long and strongly anchored and its removal requires very careful digging to avoid injury. The Wild Pink likes a deep, gravelly soil well impregnated with leaf mold and it seems to thrive most happily in light shade. When satisfied, it usually seeds itself prolifically.

The other outstanding eastern species is *S. virginica,* the Fire Pink. It bears brilliant scarlet, starry blossoms on purple-stained stems about a foot high. Both stems and leaves are slightly sticky to the touch, as is the case with so many of the race. I've not found this handsome plant an easy one to keep in the garden, though just why it should be short-lived I do not know. It objects to winter damp without doubt and should be given a ledge or little height for its home where there is a deep body of gritty soil for the roots to thrust down into. But even thus considered it frequently takes itself off after a season's spectacular performance. Usually, however, it leaves behind a batch of seedlings to console the bereaved gardener. Its natural range is from southern New Jersey to western New York and, according to Gray, from southwestern Ontario and Minnesota to many parts of the Southwest, where it haunts open, well-drained woods. It blooms later than our Wild Pink, flowering here in late May and June.

Among the western Silenes are some truly splendid beauties. *Silene californica* is one of the brilliant red species whose flowering is an achievement to give the gardener a real thrill. I have grown it here, but this year seeds from three sources over which I watched and prayed blossomed as purely pink as anything in nature could be—nice heads of small pink flowers on sticky stems about a foot high, making a great show on a bit of table-land in the rock garden, and later sowing their seed furiously all over the place—nice and very showy but, alas, not *Silene californica,* and I have no notion what it may be. The true plant, I read, is even in its prodigal home state something of a rarity, hiding high up in the mountains, generally in woodlands of Oaks and Douglas Firs. That something else is being sent out in its name is rather a pity. *S. laciniata* is another scarlet-flowered Californian, but I have not yet grown it. It is said to be very beautiful.

Silene Hookeri is an alpine of the most approved pattern—a little low plant with immense brilliant pink flowers, a huddle of downy leaves against which the deeply lobed and fimbriated salmon-colored blossoms, almost two inches across, show to supreme advantage. Not an easy plant, this, especially where the winters are apt to be mild and muggy; its only safety lies on a ledge or height where the soil, composed of grit, light loam, and chips, runs to a depth of a foot or more (granite chips are its preference) wherein the long root may thrust to its heart's content. When you receive your roots from the dealer you may feel somewhat skeptical, for more than likely they will appear like nothing so much as pieces of old wood with a few shreds adhering to them. But put them into the carefully prepared earth, and let Nature do the rest. If she is minded to go along with you, you will come to know one of the most beautiful plants that may be grown in a rock garden. But that you may fail with it again and again I am under the necessity of confessing out of my own experience. Undoubtedly the plant is perfectly hardy, but it is also undoubtedly what my old colored cook calls "peckish" and not to be satisfied with just any fare and any conditions. Mr. Purdy writes me of *S. Ingrami,* said to be similar to the above but with bright cherry-red flowers and a stronger and less sensitive constitution.

Though I have again and again, both by purchase and from seed, acquired nice little mats of *S. acaulis,* the result has always been the same—apparently entire satisfaction in its quarters but no bloom. This tiny alpine is said to be of great beauty. It is not too much to say that the fame of the race rests securely on its diminutive shoulders. What it should do is to cover its matlike surface with a glory of pink stars. With me it does nothing of the kind. It simply remains, despite all my efforts, fat and green and inscrutable. Embarrassing. Then I read that *S. elongata* resembled it in every respect save behavior. With considerable trouble I secured a plant of *S. elongata.* It has lived and thriven upon my hospitality for four years without paying so much as a single blossom in rental. It is now moved to the moraine, and if its stinginess continues its next move is to the rubbish heap.

Numerous alien Silenes seem far more responsive than our natives. The Sea Campion, for instance, *S. maritima,* is a shining example. It is an ornament for any sunny rock face, where it hangs in a soft grayish curtain and matures all through the season largish white flowers on slender stems. There is a pink form that I have not seen, and a double kind that looks like an untidy Pink. They have the typical inflated calyces and are highly satisfactory plants. They are native of Great Britain. *S. alpestris* is another delightful certainty. It is the Austrian Catchfly, native of calcareous mountains of central Europe and a charming low plant, making carpets of bright green verdure out of which materializes a foam of fringy small white flowers in late May and June, and as if this were not enough, a sprinkling throughout the rest of the summer. This is a first-rate plant for a low place in a not too sunny part of the rock garden where the soil is rich and not bone-dry. A smaller edition of it came to me as *S. a. pusilla,* very pretty and dainty. And still another of these small white starry Silenes is *S. quadrifida* (*S. quadridentata*). All belong on the cool side of the rocks and are easy to grow and to raise from seed.

If you like to grow plants that have enjoyed a long human companionship *S. Saxifraga* fills the bill. It is a slender little plant with delicate stems that rise some four or five inches high clothed with fine bright green leaves and finished with one or two flowers. These are yellowish, stained brown on the undersides, and have brownish or greenish calyces. This little Campion has been known in gardens for more than two hundred years, having been originally introduced from southern Europe.

Perhaps the best known of the family in this country is *S. Schafta,* and it seemingly has no crotchets or ineradicable likes and dislikes. It thrives where it is put, if the sun shines upon it and the soil is not waterlogged. It should make one of the first dozen rock plants tried by the beginner. Chiefly it is valuable for its bright bloom in the late summer—both bright and generous and of long duration. Perish the thought that its rosy blossoms are not quite as pure a pink as we should like, and that its foliage is somewhat excessive; our gratitude to it knows no bounds when it makes its gay appearance just when we are beginning to apologize to visitors for the flowerlessness of the rock garden and to say that they should have seen it a month ago. It quite saves the day. Years ago I grew a Campion known as *S. asterias grandiflora.* It was showy enough, sending up a foot-tall stem from a tuft of bright green leaves that carried a Scabiosa-like head of small crimson flowers. It had a somewhat common look, however, and when I found it to be short-lived I shed no tears and even went so far as to root out the seedlings it had bountifully provided.

Perhaps the two most famous Silenes from foreign parts are *S. pumilio* and *S. Elizabethae. S. pumilio,* which is by some authorities referred to *Saponaria* but is usually listed as above, is a most engaging little plant. It forms a thick mat of glabrous leaves about an inch high, and something in the way of the disobliging *acaulis.* The flowers are immense in proportion to the size of the plant and have the characteristic sticky calyces and five rather widely spaced petals, soft rose-colored and lightly crinkled at the edges. They appear in early summer, the short stems thrusting out from beneath the mat of foliage so that the flowers form a sort of wreath about the base of the plant. It is pronounced a fine moraine plant, but my three specimens appear quite happy and hearty on a sunny ledge of the rock garden. However, I shall move one into the moraine where it will get more root moisture, and we shall see what happens.

Silene Elizabethae I have never seen. I raised a splendid batch of seedlings, the seed coming from two sources, and simply trembled with anxiety while the mercury played below the zero mark last winter. But those shining tufts of leaves were untroubled and greeted the spring undiminished in health and vigor. What happened is too sad to tell. The buds formed and I quivered with anticipation. They never really opened but remained stringy half-shut calyces out of which stuck the most hideous magenta petals. Nothing more frumpish could be imagined. Here is the picture painted by Mr. Farrer of *Silene Elizabethae's* charms: late in July "forth from under the rosette stray the stems of downy claret colored velvet, wandering along the ground for a few inches and then rising like the neck of a serpent, to unfold one or two of those enormous ragged flowers that look like some monstrous Godetia gone lost among the alpine herbage." Has anyone in America had this wonderful Silene? If so, I should like to hear about it. I am still smarting from my disappointment over what came of my efforts to know it. Truly the path of the seed-sower is sown with tragedy. *Silene Elizabethae* is now referred to by some botanists as *Melandryum Elizabethae*. Perhaps under this name the true plant may be found.

This short chapter does not begin to tell the possibilities of Campion hunting. Despite disappointment it is good sport, and any time may bring to light a genuine treasure.

CHAPTER XV

THE trail of the Evening Primrose is apt to lead the seeker after knowledge concerning this charming family into a morass of confusion, albeit very pleasant confusion. As is pointed out by the late Reginald Farrer, "the family, its relationships and differences, is wrapped in impenetrable mystery, so that true, definite and finally established species are not by any means easy to come by in a group of plants as polymorphic as a range of clouds at sundown." Add to this confusing existence of several forms or types of structure in the same species or group the fact that American botanists have been having a thoroughly good time with Oenothera and have split the genus into tongue-twisting fragments, and it is readily seen that taking off from the safe platform of silence must be attended by considerable trepidation on the part of a mere amateur explorer like myself.

It is a long time since I hit the trail of the Evening Primrose, and I am still floundering about delightedly amidst a sea of baffling personalities and identities, not greatly helped by seed and plants procured from what should be the fountainhead, nor by information procured therefrom. One is in the best of company, however, as many of the great doctors disagree, and in any case an immense deal of pleasure is to be had in knowing any of these plants by whatever name they are called. Dr. Bailey in "Hortus" appreciates the difficulties that confront us and abides by the name Oenothera for the genus, giving the new names in parentheses, which is a wise provision for there is no telling when, in an excess of nomenclatural zeal, the cataloguists will espouse the changes and we should be in a bad way indeed unless fore-educated, in a manner of speaking.

Oenothera is a valuable summer flowering race, especially important to the rock gardener who seeks to keep his hills and dales colorful after the spring rush is past, as well as to the border gardener. It embraces annuals, biennials, and perennials, evening bloomers and day bloomers, which latter groups have been differentiated respectively as Evening Primroses and Sundrops. So far as I know the race, it is all American, North or South. The prevailing color of the flowers may be said to be yellow, though some of the loveliest are white and there are pinkish and reddish sorts. Many have the trick of turning from white to pink as they mature, or from yellow to red. They are sunlovers all, liking a place in dryish, well drained soil where the sun falls fully upon them. Many are lowgrowing and make ideal subjects for the rock garden where the sharp drainage is to their taste. But in severe climates a great number of them must be considered short-lived, if not actually biennial or annual. To offset this drawback it may be emphasized that they will commonly blossom the first year from seed sown early in a cold frame. The flowers of nearly all the species are large and of the most exquisite texture, compared with which it must be confessed the foliage seems a little wanting, a bit cheap. Let us get down to cases alphabetically:

Oenothera acaulis (*Oe. taraxacifolia*), the White Chilean Evening Primrose, is a delightful plant for the rock garden though it may or may not prove hardy in your locality. It, however, blossoms the first year from seed sown early. It makes a tangle of Dandelion-like leaves above which seem to float on the long slender calyx tubes an amazing succession of great flat white flowers, fragrant and gleaming, opening with the coming of dusk. The habit of the plant is decumbent and somewhat scrambling, but the effect when in full bloom is indescribably lovely. An English firm offers a form, *aurea*, which is the one I grew first, but it is inferior to the white one. The latter is said to be identical with Burbank's America, widely advertised some years ago. This species should be given the hottest and driest situation which is available.

Most of us are familiar with the tall biennial species, *Oe. biennis* (*Onagra biennis*), that clutters the roadside tangle by day with tall rag-hung stalks, but with the coming of twilight magically transforms it into a softly illumined way as the pale round moons expand suddenly. Little need be said of this Common Evening Primrose, as few will wish to grow it in their gardens. In reprisal for the many weeds sent us by the Old World we have bestowed upon it at least the Common Evening Primrose, and that so long ago that Parkinson (1729) notes its primrose color and its primrose odor, and says it was imported from Virginia. Reputed hybrids of this biennial species that long grew in my garden (they self-sow freely) are *Oe. Lamarckiana* (*Oe. biennis grandiflora*), taller of stature and with larger moons, unknown in a wild state, and Afterglow, a quite striking form whose wide yellow flowers are set off by scarlet calyces. Both of these are well worth growing in a semi-wild portion of the garden, and make of the coming of evening a quite spectacular event where they are congregated in large numbers.

An attractive low-growing, rosette-forming plant from the Southwest is *Oe. brachycarpa* (*Lavauxia brachycarpa*). The leaves are narrow and somewhat hairy and the flowers rising in a succession from the neat rosettes are about four inches across and delicately fragrant. This has proved with me a reliable hardy perennial species, and is valuable for dry, sunny, lime-impregnated slopes in the rock garden.

Oe. caespitosa (*Pachylophus caespitosa*), the Tufted Evening Primrose, or Cowboy Primrose as it is sometimes called, as I know it is a biennial (occasionally proving perennial) growing about nine inches high, with slightly downy leaves, narrow and pinnatifid, the flower buds long and pointed and opening at sundown through June and July into wide, white silken blossoms almost or quite stemless but raised above the foliage on long perianth tubes. It is one of the loveliest flowers I know and has the added grace of exquisite fragrance. As it matures the flower flushes and by morning is quite pink and faded. "A curious feature of the flower," notes Mr. Dykes, "is the prominent four-pointed stigma and the abundant yellow pollen which hangs in threads from anther to anther." I have not found it a reliable stayer in my climate though its roots may prowl about in the loose soil of the rock garden for a considerable distance, sending up little tufts here and there for several seasons. But though he may not be able to induce this plant to become a permanent resident in his garden no lover of the beautiful should fail to make its acquaintance. In some gardens it may self-sow and so become permanent, but it has not done so in mine.

Closely allied to it are *Oe. marginata* and *Oe. eximia*. The Kew Hand-List and other European authorities refer both of these species to *Oe. caespitosa,* but some American botanists give them a separate identity. Dr. Ira Gabrielson writes me concerning this confusion the following: "So far as *Oenothera marginata* and *Oe. caespitosa* are concerned, let me say that some of the more conservative botanists consider them identical or at least simply forms of the same plant. So far as I can see, for garden purposes, they are the same, the chief difference being that *caespitosa* is uniformly covered with short silvered hairs, while *marginata* is particularly hairy on the margins and the ribs of the leaves. I cannot help you any on *Oe. eximia,* because the plant happens to come from a territory with which I am not too familiar. It is, however, one of the same closely knit group which contains *caespitosa*. Perhaps the basis for the difference of these plants is the extreme variability of their leaf shape. In some specimens of *caespitosa,* for example, the leaves are almost entire, and in others deeply scalloped and cut, after the fashion of dandelion leaves. If one saw only a few plants of one form that happened to have entire leaves and a few plants of another species that happened to be deeply cut, it would be easy to get the impression that this character was a distinctive one. However, all Primroses of this type do vary tremendously in shape of leaf and general habit of growth."

Rydberg gives the locale of *caespitosa* as dry hills, Saskatchewan—Nebraska—New Mexico—Montana; of *eximia,* as hills and banks, South Dakota —New Mexico; of *marginata,* as hills, Idaho—Colorado—Utah—Oregon. So the identity of your plants may possibly be somewhat determined by the locality from which you, or its vender, derived it. I am sure in the several times I have raised it from seed I have always had the same lovely thing, and, whatever it is, it was wholly satisfying from the standpoint of beauty. It is obvious that all these plants require dry, well drained, sunlit situations, preferably in a rock garden.

Oe. Clutei, a new species discovered in Arizona by Willard Clute, I have not grown. It is reported a biennial, making a large rosette of leaves the first season, and in the second throwing up a four-foot stalk flanked by lesser stalks and bearing in quantity yellow flowers four inches across that open out flat. No doubt a desirable plant and one of which seed is to be had.

A group of good hardy perennial kinds for the borders comprises *Oe. fruticosa (Kneiffia fruticosa)* and its varieties *major* and *Youngii,* and *Oe. glauca (Kneiffia glauca)* with its varieties *Fraseri* and *Eldorado.* These are anybody's plants, hardy, spready, gay in their bright yellow summer blossoming, and happy in any sunny border. *Oe. fruticosa* belongs to the Carolinas and the region out through Ohio, Michigan, and Idaho. Its height is about eighteen inches, erect and stocky, and the calyces and outside of the tube and the stem are tinged with red, which in the improved forms is accentuated and adds much to the showiness of the plants.

Oe. glauca belongs to the mountains of Virginia, Kentucky, etc., and a good deal resembles the foregoing save that it is somewhat less in stature and the leaves are glaucous. The variety *Eldorado* is said to be semi-double and a little taller than the type, but I have had no experience with it. Like all the others of this group it is sub-shrubby. All these *fruticosa* and *glauca* forms are day-flowering and make a most attractive showing for several weeks in the summer. No plants could be more easily grown.

Then we have *Oe. missouriensis* (*Oe. macrocarpa, Megapterium missouriense*), the Ozark Sundrop, a yellow night-flowering species of importance for the edge of a sunny border or the rock garden. The plant is somewhat lax and trailing, the leaves bright green and narrow, the flowers wide yellow suns that continue to materialize all through the summer. This plant belongs to the limestone cliffs and barrens of Montana to Nebraska, Colorado and southward. It is a good subject for the rock garden, for the plant is no more than nine inches high, though it has a considerable spread. In any case it keeps its neighborhood blossomy well into the autumn. It requires full sunshine and a well drained soil.

Oe. pumila—or so I know it—is a little species with the smallest flowers of the genus, only a few inches tall, a trifle weedish in appearance but yielding a succession of day-flowering, yellow, penny-sized blooms all through the summer and fall. Its flat rosettes occupy little space, and it may be given a place in some sunny, sandy locality for the sake of its continuous bloom. And now we come to three of the beauties of the race with which we must bring this discourse to a close, though we have hardly touched the fringes of the garment that is, or was, Oenothera.

From Montana west and south we derive *Oe. speciosa* (*Hartmannia speciosa*), a hardy perennial that was one of the first plants to teach me that one can have too much of a good thing—for it is a plant of hungry ambition. But it is lovely. Somewhat shrubby and growing laxly erect to a height of about fourteen inches, it clothes itself in somewhat hairy leaves and a gossamer flutter of white blossoms about three inches across that are delicately fragrant at night and make the characteristic change to pink before twenty-four hours are out. It is a day-bloomer and never fails to evoke admiration from those who see it. A pink-flowered form offered as *rosea* or *rubra* is said to be more compact in habit. Give it a soil sandy in quality and full sun, and you will satisfy all its needs.

Oe. tetraptera (*Hartmannia tetraptera*) is a night-blooming biennial of great charm with white, thin-textured flowers opening punctually at sundown. I grow it in the rock garden, where it self-sows freely but never attains the twenty-two inches allowed it by authorities, nor is it fragrant. Dr. Bailey gives as synonyms *Oe. Childsii* and *Oe. Sarrazinii*, and says it is found wild in Arizona and Texas, as well as in South

America. It blossoms from midsummer well into the autumn.

Tried for the first time this past season, and proving to be a most lovely thing, is the Desert Primrose, *Oe. trichocalyx* (*Onagra trichocalyx*). It is biennial or at best a short-lived perennial. Seeds started in a cold frame in December, 1932, flowered all through the summer and autumn of 1933. On a plain of the rock garden it proved rather an ungainly plant in habit, but when the immense fragrant white flowers began their evening performance any lack in grace was forgiven it. The flowers are of silken texture and filled at the heart with golden stamens. Dr. Ira Gabrielson says, "From the Dalles of the mighty Columbia eastward, the sand dunes and cliffs alike are banked knee-deep in tangled masses of this fragrant Evening Primrose." When I covered the garden late in the autumn some plants seemed to have disappeared, others were still showing points of growth. I do not yet know what the winter will do to them, but as it blossoms so readily from seed sown the same season any one may enjoy this exquisite newcomer.

CHAPTER XVI

IT IS the mission, or perhaps we should say the destiny, of certain plants, as it is of certain persons, to make the world in which they live a pleasanter and more gracious place, not by means of conspicuous achievements or outstanding personality, but by means of more subtle, less dramatic attributes. In the garden's scheme such plants are fully as important as those of more striking aspect. Indeed it is such as these that often endow a garden with peculiar charm, not always easily analyzed but certainly felt. Like mist in the distance they soften and enhance the landscape, round off the angles, bestow grace and a little sense of mystery where perhaps without them would be brittle contrast and harsh outlines.

As I consider this type of plant there come to mind *Gypsophila paniculata* and its several forms; Artemisia Silver King and *A. Stelleriana; Valeriana officinalis,* with heads of silver-gray lace; certain Corydalis, lovely in shadowed walls; the Sea Lavenders or Statice, now known as Limonium; many kinds of Columbines; and especially the Thalictrums. It is these last named plants, commonly called Meadowrues, that we have here especially under consideration, first because they do not seem to receive due regard in gardens, and second because they ask so little of us in return for what they do for us. They are easy to grow, enduring, full of charm.

They are a genus of some magnitude, the Thalictrums; some fifty species are known, but only a small number of these are at present in cultivation. They are to be found growing naturally over a large part of the Temperate and Arctic regions of Europe, Asia, and North America, with a few species in the Andes of South America. And they belong to the Buttercup family, the natural order Ranunculaceae, with which to the non-botanical eye they seem to have no affinity, and they are first cousins of the Anemones. Among them are to be found kinds suited to the borders, to the wild garden and the waterside, to woodland and to the rock garden. A truly versatile race! And unless we except *Thalictrum dipterocarpum,* one of the latest introductions, none of them presents any great difficulty to the cultivator.

The foliage of the Meadowrues is their chief fortune. Save in a few cases the flowers are inconspicuous, the sepals falling so quickly that the flower seems to be all stamens. The foliage, however, is uniformly beautiful. In fact I know of no race of plants that is so generously endowed with lovely greenery. And it has the advantage of remaining lovely through the season.

The most showy Thalictrums, if such gossamer, ethereal things can ever be characterized as showy, are for the most part of European and Asiatic origin. The latest to come into cultivation is the most impressive when well grown. It was introduced from high altitudes in western China by the late E. H. Wilson, and seems not to be easily dealt with in lowland gardens, for it is seldom seen in a flourishing condition. It is evidently not everybody's plant. We cannot all give it the conditions which it must have to make it the thing of incomparable grace and color that it is when perfectly contented. Much experimenting with it a number of years ago taught me that it desires a very rich soil, rich with good farmyard manure. It will not, I am sure, thrive in acid soil or even where the soil is neutral. Drainage is another requisite; in heavy, clogged soils it dies off in winter, and even succumbs when we have spells of moist, muggy heat. Yet it needs moisture, and in dry weather should be faithfully watered every few days. In winter it should be protected north of Philadelphia with a blanket of leaves or litter. Its position should be out in the sunshine, never beneath the drip of trees, or crowded by hungry shrubs. Plant it, if you are not by now discouraged, in the spring, and enjoy this graceful plant that sends sturdy stems aloft to a height of six feet or more, and in August breaks forth in a mist of rosy-lavender blossoms set off by sulphur-colored stamens that are lovely indeed above the characteristic Meadowrue foliage, which in this case is of a glaucous tone. There is a white-flowering form offered but I have not seen it.

Thalictrum Delavayi is almost as lovely and somewhat easier to grow. It also is a Chinese plant but more slender and not nearly so tall as *T. dipterocarpum*, with purplish stems and a haze of lavender blossoms. For some reason this fine species seems to have been dropped from American dealers' lists—at least I am unable to find it; but seeds are to be had, and all the Thalictrums come easily from seed. *T. Delavayi* likes a moist position and, as it grows little more than two feet tall, might find a place in a spacious rock garden. Neither of these two species is really "easy," but when did difficulties to be overcome ever deter a gardener who really had the right stuff in him!

The most frequently planted Meadowrues in this country are *T. aquilegifolium* and its various forms. They flower in June and are most useful in softening the effects of that prodigal month. The stems are purplish and hollow, and the young plant as it makes its appearance in early spring might be mistaken for a Columbine. It is beautiful and kind, thriving in any border that is not too poor and parched, but responding gratefully to a sound, strong loam in a sunny position. I believe the type form has flattened panicles of greenish yellow flowers, but this is not often seen, nor would it come off well in competition with the forms known as *roseum* and *atropurpureum*, or even with the white form. All these are lovely, breaking above their charming Columbine foliage into broad masses of feathery flowers, or rather stamens, for the sepals fall almost immediately. The height is from three to four feet.

When Delphiniums bloom I am always glad of a mass of one or other of the yellow-flowered Thalictrums to stand by them. These are admirable and useful garden plants and not difficult to please. The most lovely is *T. glaucum.* It grows from four to five feet tall and has perhaps the most beautiful foliage in the family. The stems are stout enough to uphold their burden of pale yellow mistlike bloom without staking. This yellow bloom is lovely with the gray leaves that remain in good condition through the season. Many uses may be found for this plant. One I like especially, besides the usual Delphinium companionship: it makes a most effective and softening background for the crude color of Herring Lilies, *Lilium croceum*.

Taller and with smaller leaves and less effective yellow inflorescence is *T. flavum* that blooms a little later than the above and may be put to the same uses. The foliage is delicate and beautiful, but the plant requires to be staked. It is said to thrive by the waterside, and it also grows well under favorable garden conditions. A third yellow-flowered form is offered in this country, but I do not know it. It is said to be a hybrid, a creation of the great Lemoine, and grows five feet tall, blossoming in July and August, thus following the two foregoing yellow-flowered species. It sounds worth while as it is said to bear "immense panicles of charming sulphur-yellow flowers." Its name is *T. sulfureum*.

Of the native kinds there are several worth growing and one or two that might be called showy. Most country-wise persons know the tall Meadowrue, *Thalictrum polygamum*, found spreading a pale mist in wet meadows and along stream-sides from July to September, from Newfoundland to Ohio and southwards. Though a plant naturally addicted to moist places it is thoroughly accommodating, transplanting easily to borders or wild gardens where the soil is rich. Ordinarily about four feet in height, it is known under

certain conditions to grow much taller. Its wide
feathery flower masses are white, rarely purplish, the
panicles very compound. It is a cool and pretty thing
for summer borders. *T. purpurascens* (*T. revoluti*) is
especially to be recommended for its pale graceful foliage. Under favorable conditions this species is known
to grow six feet tall. The inflorescence consists of a
drooping mass, a foot across, of mauve flowers, not
conspicuous but very telling in their softening influence
on their more strident neighbors. On sultry days it
emits a somewhat heavy odor. *T. purpurascens* is
found in rocky woods and along stream-sides from Massachusetts to New Jersey and westward.

And now we come to the kinds suitable for use in
the rock garden. The choicest among the native species
is the little Rue Anemone, *Thalictrum anemonoides*,
that is also known as *Anemonella thalictroides*. It is a
fragile and lovely wilding, graciously common in thin
moist woods from southern New Hampshire over a
large part of the country. It is often found in the
company of the Windflower, *Anemone quinquefolia*,
which it superficially resembles, but from which it may
always be distinguished by the fact that, whereas the
true Anemone bears a solitary flower on each slender
stem, the Rue Anemone boasts two or three white or
pale pink flowers with golden stamens. The characteristic leaves are olive-green in groups of three, and the
light stem rises from a little cluster of thickened tuberous roots to a height of only a few inches. It is easy to
transplant from the woods to your rock garden, or it may
be purchased from dealers in wild flowers—a sweet and
airy addition to the spring display.

The Meadowrues for Feathery Grace

Another native that should not be neglected, though its blossoms have no value, is *T. dioicum,* called the Early Meadowrue. If one wants foliage of uncommon beauty in any odd corner of the rock garden or Fern border, this easily grown plant will supply it, the smooth, pale green leaves on slender spreading branches making their appearance in early spring. It should be planted in masses in woodsy soil. This species is common in rocky woods from central Maine westward and southward, and is sometimes mistaken for Maidenhair Fern.

Two little fellows of alien origin should not be forgotten when we are scouting for the rock garden. These are *T. alpinum* and *T. minus* and its several forms.

T. alpinum is a modest little plant in appearance, "not easy," says a British writer, "to catch sight of in the highlands of the Alps, whether of England, Scotland or Europe." Nor is it so easy to grow. Its leaves are grayish and arranged in a lacelike pattern, and its tasselly inflorescence is rather greenish yellow, not important. The leaves are the point. It makes a little display, pale and ethereal, and no more than four or five inches high, but pretty enough for a place in the moraine or a bed of "strong, gritty peat." It is not a plant for just any corner in the rock garden. It wants consideration from eye and hand.

T. minus, also of European origin, is found in rocky districts and is variable in habit. Perhaps the prettiest is called *T. m. adiantifolium* that grows about eighteen inches tall, sometimes less, is bushy in habit with very fine bluish green foliage that is nice for cutting or veiling an uninteresting corner. It is very easy to grow in any rocky situation that is not too bone-dry.

Even quite a small garden might find reason and space for all these Meadowrues. They pay their way whether in or out of bloom.

CHAPTER XVII

HOLLYHOCK COUSINS

NOWADAYS when we are asking plants to grow and blossom with somewhat less attention than they have enjoyed of yore, the Mallow clan presents itself for consideration with most authentic qualifications. What have we been thinking of during the more golden years to neglect them almost entirely! They are lovely, accommodating, infinitely useful for border or wild garden, and for cutting. What more could a distracted gardener ask? Moreover, they belong to July chiefly, that month of inevitable let-down and laissez-faire which is so trying to the soul of the careful gardener.

The Mallows are members of the order Malvaceae that includes the Rose of Sharon, the Abutilon of pots, the wild Marsh Mallow, *Althaea officinalis,* which though so delightful and common a feature of our salt marshes, is an alien naturalized from Europe. But we are here concerned with certain herbaceous ornamentals, perennial and annual, embracing Malope, Althaea, Lavatera, Sidalcea, Malva, Malvastrum and the bright little Callirhoë.

Chief of these is the Hollyhock, *Althaea rosea,* which has been sung and praised and pictured in all its attitudes and phases since it was introduced from the Orient about 1573, but which is somewhat put out of counte-

nance today by newer and less meritorious introductions.
It is the saving grace in the garden of many a beginner,
for it is striking, colorful, picturesque, reliable, and it
should be no less the pride of more established gardens
as it was in Parkinson's in the early sixteenth century.
He says it "is not found but in gardens euery where,"
so he seems not to have known of its Oriental origin.

Hollyhocks come double or single; some people like
best the tight powder-puff blossoms set in a circle of
smooth guard petals, spaced primly along tall erect
spires, and some prefer the simpler single kinds. Both
kinds run to lovely colors—all the pinks, reds, prunes,
mauves, yellows, and white, but no blues. One may
choose the colors carefully to fit into a preconceived
color scheme, or grow them carelessly massed, all colors, and achieve an effect of old-fashioned chintz that
is very charming. Some delightful combinations are
possible, too, such as pale pink and lemon-colored varieties, or some of the dusky prune or maroon kinds
with bright cerise ones. In a border where early white
Phlox, Lemon Lilies, and *Campanula lactiflora* pre-
dominate, yellow and white Hollyhocks are an addition.
A Lemon Lily which fits into this scheme admirably
is the new Hemerocallis F. A. Crawford, which has a
charming starry form and delicate fragrance.

Hollyhocks are best grown at the back of the borders
in irregular groups; or they may be allowed to for-
gather in unserried ranks, as one so often sees them in
country gardens, behind a white picket fence. Hollyhocks and white picket fences have an especial affinity
for each other. *Althaea ficifolia*, the Fig-leaved or
Antwerp Hollyhock (originally from Siberia), is a de-

lightful single-flowered kind, not quite so tall as and more freely branching than the offspring of *Althaea rosea*. Its flowers are of lovely form and a clear pale yellow in color, but if it is allowed to grow near Hollyhocks of other colors seedlings spring up, displaying the most charming hues—apricot, amber, cream, salmon, flame, and the like. And I have found these Fig-leaved kinds very long-lived and very much less prone to attacks of the dread rust which far too often disfigures the other kinds. Sprayings of Bordeaux Mixture repeated several times early in the season are recommended for this disease, but I have found the most certain protection is *youth*. I never keep a plant of the ordinary Hollyhock more than two years. Like all the Mallow tribe, they are easily raised from seed, and if the old plants are ruthlessly pulled out and burned there will be little trouble with rust. For the rest, light and a free circulation of air and a deeply dug soil, not too rich, are all they demand.

Named Hollyhocks are not common in this country, but one may procure seed of lovely kinds; and it is surprising how close they come to the originals. Newport Pink is a lovely double pink sort, its color pure and its habit very fully double. Orange Prince is another fine named sort of an unusual blend of orange and apricot. Both these kinds grow tall and strong and are well worth having. Chater's doubles are very opulent and fine, as are the strains known as "Triumph" that has waved and fringed flowers in a bewildering variety of hues, and "Imperator" whose flowers of many tints are composed of a very broad collar of frilled and fringed petals with a large double center rosette.

What Happens in My Garden

Of course Hollyhocks must be firmly staked if their stately port is to be maintained. A strong bamboo stake four feet above ground should be sufficient for the tallest kinds, leaving the upper length of the stalk to assume a graceful pose.

While the Hollyhock is undoubtedly queen of its tribe, some of its cousins are of passing charm. My favorite is the Musk Mallow, and the white Musk Mallow for choice, *Malva moschata*. These are British wild flowers, but according to Gray are to be met with in our wild in certain localities. They grow about two feet tall, bloom prodigally throughout July and August, and sometimes into September, and the wide flaring blossoms borne in quick succession at the ends of the branches have a fine satin finish that is very attractive. The leaves are cut and cut again, and the plant has a nice bushy, space-filling habit. It was Miss Jekyll who suggested the cool and charming association of white Musk Mallows and steel-blue Eryngiums, one of the most pleasing of summer companionships. And I have found both the pink and the white kinds delightful when grown behind lavender and white Stokesias.

Malva Alcea, too, is attractive, taller than the Musk Mallow, deeper in hue, and the cut leaves a little downy, the whole plant more spready and a trifle more rampant, the blossoms somewhat bell-shaped. It blooms later, also, its heyday being in August, and I have found it hardy where the Musk Mallow succumbed.

I do not know why through many years of trying out every plant I could lay hands on I did not, until a few years ago, meet with the Sidalceas. I saw them first in the lovely garden of Mrs. Frederic Beebe at Swamp-

[150]

scott, Massachusetts, and fell an immediate victim to their charms. Like all the Mallow tribe known to me, they flower in the full summer, and have a generous period of bloom. *Sidalcea candida,* a native of the Rocky Mountains, and its mallow-pink form are perennial but should be often renewed from seed as they are not long-lived, though they persist longer in a light warm soil than in a heavy cold medium. They are profuse with their flowering and bear their round blossoms on slender stems two or three feet high, which makes them useful for cutting. Sidalcea Rose Queen is thought an improved form of the common pink Sidalcea, and several firms offer hybrids that embrace a color range from pink through salmon, rose, mauve, and heliotrope. These must be very charming, but I have not seen them. Rosy Gem grows only about eighteen inches tall and might conceivably be grown in a large rock garden where height is desirable. The Sidalceas belong to our West country, and the name Prairie Mallow is far more appropriate to them than the more often used Greek Mallow, which would seem to have no reason at all. They are found along streams and in dampish meadows in Wyoming, New Mexico, and Utah. There are numerous species out through the West which might well repay investigation.

A beautiful annual Mallow is *Lavatera trimestris,* a plant from the Mediterranean region, more used abroad than in this country. The large flaring flowers are a fine silvery pink color and there is a satin-white form that is also lovely. Both these are offered in improved forms by seedsmen as *L. splendens rosea* and *L. splendens alba.* They may be sown under glass early in the year and later transplanted to where they are to grow, but I have found they have an unaccountable way of damping off unless weather conditions are just to their mind, and the more certain method is to sow the seed thinly where it is wanted in the borders and to thin out the seedlings to a foot or more apart. They make fine bushy plants and blossom all through the late summer and autumn, creating a fine show towards the back of a border with annual Larkspurs in blue and violet in front, or tall Ageratum.

A lower-growing annual Mallow is *Malope grandiflora*, bearing in profusion bright or pale rose or white flowers. These seem little used nowadays, which seems a pity as they are very gay and pretty where a quick and long-lasting show is desired. Malope does not like a starved soil, however, and will not do its best save where the earth has been deeply dug and generously enriched, and where it is given plenty of elbow room. So considered, and well watered in dry weather, the plants reach a height of about two feet and bloom all summer and into the autumn. They may be sown indoors in February or out of doors in late April.

A tall annual plant having a certain foliage value is *Malva crispa*, the Curled Mallow, or what Parkinson called the French Mallow. Many Mallows grew in Parkinson's garden, including this French Mallow, which, by the way, was not French in origin but came from Syria. It was popular in those old days as a pot herb and was also used medicinally, especially, according to the forthright Parkinson, "when there is cause to moue the belly downwards, which by his slippery qualities it doth helpe forward."

Hollyhock Cousins

Once when I was in England *Lavatera Olbia* was in all the gardens, a showy plant, shrubby at the base and tall enough to earn the name of Tree Mallow. It is an old plant in European gardens, being native in Provence, but it is not hardy in our northern latitudes; nor need we sigh overmuch on account of it, for as I remember the flowers they were somewhat more on the magenta side than is pleasing save with careful placing. Seeds of it may be started early under glass and will bloom before the summer has gone far.

And now to speak of two little Mallows of our West country, *Malvastrum coccineum* and *Callirhoë involucrata*, the latter easily raised from seed. It is a sprawling little plant, spreading vigorously in dry and sunny places and bearing innumerable small Mallow flowers of the most unashamed and flaunting magenta of any plant I ever saw. "Thumbs down!" cry the magenta haters, but believe me, this small Poppy Mallow, as it is called, is a very good subject in an unwanted place, valiant in its cheerfulness through all sorts of exigencies and brightening the corner where it grows in quite the right spirit, if not with quite the right color. After a summer spent in Europe I quite unexpectedly found myself with a gravel path of the Poppy Mallow, which had moved during my absence from the less congenial rich soil of the border into the dry gravel path. Grown at the top of a dry wall the Poppy Mallow is very well placed. It flings its branches about in the sunshine in exuberant well-being, trailing over the edge in untidy but effective drapery, and blossoming inexhaustibly from early summer until autumn. In the rock garden it must be more carefully placed, for it is no respecter of small royalties and its color does shout; but a sunny rock face down which it may sprawl gives it scope for its activities, and against the gray stone its color is beautiful.

The Flame Mallow, *Malvastrum coccineum,* is quite different. Its color is as vibrant—a splendid apricot-orange—but will be offensive to none. It is a fine subject for a sunny rock garden, a stony slope suiting it exactly where the roots may run about among the stones, and where its five-parted gray leaves and short spikes of flaming blossoms show to perfection. "Prairie Fire" would be a good name for it, for when it is in bloom it has all the appearance of a small conflagration licking its way among the stones. It is quite hardy and one of the most satisfactory plants I have yet had from the Far West.

Plants suffer from the vagaries of fashion as do other worthy objects, and just now the Mallow clan is not, so to speak, in the public eye. Hollyhocks are thought "too obvious" by the esthetic, the Musk Mallows not sufficiently what the catalogues call "elegant." But all these plants are friendly and blossomy when these attributes are most wanted.

CHAPTER XVIII

DREAMS are half of gardening, perhaps the better half, for there is nearly always, however we may ignore it, "a worm i' the bud" of realization. "If" is the little word that is the open sesame to dreams, and so I use it here. If, then, among my landed possessions I numbered a gently shelving bank open to the sun and of generous dimensions, I should devote it to the wild Roses of the world, as many as I could get together. Nature holds nothing more enchanting in her capacious basket than her wild Roses, yet they are very generally neglected for the sake of other shrubs. As a matter of fact, when we think of shrubs Roses do not commonly come to mind at all; such as Lilacs, Forsythias, Mock Oranges in their great variety fill the vision. Yet the wild bush Roses are none the less shrubs and possess a most uncommon charm. Indeed the charm of many of them may be said to be fourfold, for not a few possess lovely flowers, handsome fruits, attractive foliage as well as a sweet fragrance. They do not storm our senses with flamboyant and heady scents as do the Azaleas, whose blossoming they follow, with great fragrant plumes as do the Lilacs, with sweet ivory wreaths as the Mock Oranges, or with the golden showers of the Forsythias. But a bank of free-growing wild Roses in its heyday presents a billowing softness of contour, a wash of tender color that cannot fail to charm the sensitive observer. And at no time of the year is it unworthy of careful observation. Even in winter it offers snatches of color for the eye to feast upon, for many of the long canes will then be found to be richly colored and the hips provide a gay second blossoming against the snow.

Alas, I have no such providential sunny bank, and so I have been constrained during the many years of my gardening life to grow the wild Roses about the garden in the motley of other shrubs, and to treasure the memory of others that I have not grown but have met with by the roadside and in fields, in botanic gardens and arboretums, in private gardens here and there.

Nature has been generous with Roses. They are distributed over a wide area of the earth's surface. North America is particularly rich in them, the continents of Europe and Asia as well. Of late years China has proved a treasure house of new species. Two great plant hunters of our day, the late E. H. Wilson and the late Reginald Farrer, introduced a great many for which the Rose-loving world will long be grateful.

Intimate acquaintance with the wild Roses sometimes induces a slight contempt for the pruned and pampered beauties of the Rose garden; in the process of such meticulous culture and currying as they are subjected to they seem to have lost some inherent quality of charm, a sort of pristine freshness, that the wild Rose has kept, and for which the more opulent air and corpulent contours of the "manufactured" Rose do not

wholly compensate. Generally speaking, too, the wild
Roses are of stronger constitution than the hybrids
and thus less susceptible to the many ills to which the
more highly bred flesh is heir. They are not indifferent to good soil but flourish very well in something
quite ordinary; and they ask little in the way of prun-
ing, only to be freed of dead or crowding wood and occasionally to have the tips of the canes snipped back
where they are outgrowing their allotted situation. Sun
and free wind they must have, and it is little enough to
give them in return for what they give us.

As to hues, we have among them many tones of
cream, yellow, blush, pink, rose and red, as well as pure
white. The flowers are nearly always single and borne
in large or small clusters, though occasionally solitary.
The foliage is often distinctive and beautiful, sometimes grayish or ruddy, and frequently assumes brilliant autumn coloration. The habit of the wild Rose
shrubs with their long curving canes is graceful and
decorative. Some are true bushes and require to be
spaced accordingly; some are climbers and make their
way upwards narrowly between other shrubs; some
are Tiny Tims for the rock garden. It is mainly of the
shrubby sorts that I wish here to speak. The kinds
small enough for use in the rock garden are mentioned
in the chapter devoted to dwarf-growing shrubs.

On our very doorsteps we have a number of Roses
that are of no common sort yet are certainly not generally grown in gardens. To make a collection of native
species alone would be a well rewarded task. The
Michigan or Prairie Rose, *Rosa setigera,* because it is
a climber (our only native climber) perhaps has no

place in this chapter; but it is a lovely thing and, placed at the top of a bank, may be grown as a bush, its long branches trailing far downwards. In certain sections of the East where it has been cultivated in gardens, this Rose has run out of bounds and is to be met with sprawling over stone line fences or weaving through the roadside tangle of trees and shrubs, conspicuous because of its generous clusters of pale or deep pink single blossoms with prominent styles, and the fact that it commonly has only three leaflets, though sometimes five. It is a parent of the Rose Baltimore Belle—a very famous and typical belle of the eighteen hundreds, blushing but entirely able to look after herself, tradition to the contrary notwithstanding.

Those who know the rocky character of the New England countryside are familiar too with the Meadow, or Early Wild Rose, *Rosa blanda.* They will remember the bland pink hue of its flowers borne singly or sometimes in threes, its crowding, reddish, thornless stems and in the late summer and autumn its round red hips. This is a low-growing kind, perhaps to four feet, suckering freely, so that it makes an effective planting towards the base of the Rose bank or forward in any group of shrubbery. It is very hardy. *R. arkansana,* the Arkansas Rose, is a good deal like it in appearance and habit; but as I grow it here on a hillock of the rock garden which it is slowly taking possession of, it is of dwarfer stature and the flowers are much more fragrant, and it frequently blooms again after its June display.

A still dwarfer-growing species is *R. nitida,* the Northeastern Rose. This also is very hardy and though found on the borders of swamps and in such like dampish

[158]

places does well as a border plant. It is one of our most lovely wild Roses and has a distinguished appearance in any company. Its flowers are a charming pink color, its red, eighteen-inch stems thickly beset with slender spines, its foliage narrow and glossy and turning brightly with the coming of autumn. The hips commonly hang all winter, defying winter gloom and cold. Like the foregoing, this Rose suckers freely and makes a fine foreground planting or an effective banding for walks or drives.

Rosa lucida has broader leaves, and the flowers are sweet and perhaps of a deeper hue than those of *R. nitida.* It suckers little but makes an erect bush from three to five feet tall, bearing its flowers singly. In the dark seasons it offers for our cheer its pleasant reddy-brown stems and many gay hips. Beguiling as are our native Roses, one must get on, and I mention but two more. The Pasture Rose, *R. humilis,* commonly low-growing, but occasionally reaching a height of six feet under favorable conditions, has an erect and bushy habit and bears fragrant flowers over a long period in early summer. This species will stand some shade if necessary, and it is extremely hardy. It is also one of the species the foliage of which turns brilliantly in autumn. The Swamp or Carolina Rose is one of the commonest of our wild Roses, growing to a height of from five to seven feet and suckering freely. It bears its wide pink flowers in corymbose clusters. The hips cling all winter and keep their color until early spring.

Of course the Sweetbrier, *R. Eglanteria,* is a tramp and a most ingratiating one. Starting in Europe, it has wandered half the world over. We meet it as an old friend on the edges of New England pastures or in Virginia lanes, as well as on the other side of the water, tall, thorny, bespangled in season with pale, almost scentless blooms, but eternally endeared to us for the keen sweetness of its leaves that is released by the pressure of the fingers, by rain or frost. In any collection it should be present, as should the Dog Rose, *R. canina*, often its companion in our wild, though also of European origin. This is a pretty kind possessed of awkward elegance, and its single blooms are fragrant, though its leaves are not. Both these species are tall and bend this way and that seeking support.

Of all the Roses that have come to us from overseas in late years, none has so firmly established itself in our regard as has *Rosa Hugonis*. It is a wreath Rose, that is to say it bears its single canary-yellow blossoms thickly along the curving branches so that each branch suggests a wreath. The foliage is small and elegant, the bush about five feet tall, and even when leafless the slender brown stems have a certain distinction. It is one of the earliest Roses to bloom, and the yellow flowers are followed by black hips. *Rosa Hugonis* was introduced from China some thirty or more years ago by a Reverend Father whose name it bears.

Appearing a good deal like a double-flowered *Hugonis* is another yellow Rose, *R. xanthina*, from northern China and Korea. If well suited as to situation it is more vigorous than the foregoing and blooms for a long period. It has small delicate foliage and the early blossoming that recommends its compatriot. Both flower before the two yellow Roses with which we are

more familiar, *Rosa Harisonii* and the Persian Yellow
Rose, each of which makes a charming shrub for use in
borders or as specimens. One more yellow-flowered
Rose may be mentioned, *R. Ecae,* from Afghanistan
and Turkestan. It is little known but is quite hardy,
the bush growing from four to five feet tall with finely
divided foliage that has the fragrance in some degree
of the Sweetbrier.

I have always loved the Scotch or Burnet Rose,
R. spinosissima, in its various forms. They make
tangled bushes some five feet tall that sucker freely,
so that the many fine-spined stems soon form broad
masses. There are white, pink, and pale yellow forms,
and one that I have grown ever since I had a garden
is called Stanwell Perpetual. It bears small, double,
flesh-pink flowers with a subtle fragrance in the greatest profusion, and while certainly not perpetual does
now and again yield a nosegay out of season. Mr. Wilson's favorite in the group is the variety *altaica* from
the Altai Mountains of Siberia. "It is more vigorous,"
he says, "than its sisters, growing fully six feet tall
with pure white flowers, each two inches across, abun-
dantly produced." The fruits of all the *spinosissima*
Roses are black.

One of Mr. Wilson's most important introductions
is the lovely Rose he named for his wife—*Helenae.* It
is said that the white blossoms perfume the countryside in central China during its flowering. *R. Helenae*
is a strong-growing plant, making canes from six to
twelve feet in length that arch gracefully and along
which the flowers are borne in large clusters. The hips
are orange-colored. Mr. Wilson is also responsible for

the introduction of the beautiful and distinctive *R. Moyesii,* which when growing in good limy soil may reach a height of nine feet; but it is said to be somewhat difficult to establish. The dark leaves are grayish on the undersides, and the flowers, nearly three inches across, are usually produced singly and are of an unusual tone of dark rose-red, set off by a boss of golden stamens. The fruits are conspicuous, bright orange-scarlet, and shaped like a bottle. A slender, delicate-leaved species with fruits of the same shape as the foregoing is *R. Sweginzowi,* introduced by Mr. Farrer. The flowers are pink in clusters.

In its typical form the Mount Omei Rose, *R. omeiensis,* has lovely feathery foliage and white four-petaled flowers that appear early. The curious pear-shaped fruits are red with yellow bases and stems and make a lively display in themselves. There is another form with all-yellow fruits that is said to be otherwise identical with the type, and there are several other forms offered, one which is said to have "immense thorns whose broad wing-like bases almost join along the branches, making a very unique and striking effect."

Two Chinese species worth including in a collection are *R. Willmottiae,* named by Mr. Wilson for Miss Willmott of Warley Place, and *R. setipoda.* The first makes a dense bush some six to eight feet in height clothed with fine and very ornamental foliage and bearing many solitary lilac-pink flowers, followed by orange-red fruits. The effect of the plant is slender and elegant, the stems somewhat drooping and of a grayish hue. *R. setipoda* grows tall also, and in June is gay with many-flowered clusters of large pink flowers that

pale somewhat towards the centers; and it is almost
as gay when later in the season the polished scarlet
bottle-shaped fruits have matured.

Perhaps the most beautiful of Europe's wild Roses
is *R. rubrifolia;* that is, it is the most beautiful from
the point of view of its unusual foliage. The purplish
leaves and stems seem to be overlaid with a glaucescent
bloom and are unique in the Rose world. Its starry,
bright pink blooms show delightfully against the setting
made by the foliage. This species stands out with real
distinction in any group of shrubs or as a specimen,
giving a good account of itself the year through, for
when the foliage has fallen we are still attracted by
the darkly tinged stems, particularly against snow.
R. rubrifolia reaches a height of about six feet. It is
native in the mountains of central and southern Europe.

The Rugosa Roses, sometimes called Hedgehog, or
Ramanas Rose, make ideal shrubs. Many changes have
been rung on the original Rugosa Rose that was introduced from the Orient in 1845, and while we still have
many varieties that show the compact, somewhat stiff
upright growth, and the wrinkled, disease-proof leaves
of the type with its richly fragrant, wide, rather flimsy
single blooms of an indefinite magenta hue or pure
white, we now have also numerous longer-limbed varieties of which Conrad F. Meyer, with its enormous
double-cupped flowers carried on canes ten feet high,
is a good example. The less tall and very hardy sport
Blanc Double de Coubert is the best double pure white
Rugosa, most lovely in the bud and very fragrant. This
has the foliage and general habit of the type. An exquisite white kind also is Madame Georges Bruant,

with loosely assembled pure white flowers having petals thin almost as tissue borne in clusters, and a delicious fragrance. It blooms continuously. Agnes, the new and only yellow Rugosa, I have not seen, but it sounds attractive, copper in the bud, opening to pale gold, very double, and sweet-scented. The foliage is said to be gray and very wrinkled.

The Rugosa Roses are unrivaled for hedges, screens, or for any purpose where a hardy, healthy, free-flowering shrub is wanted. There will be no disappointment where they are used. The profusely borne sealing-wax-red hips are not the least of their attractions.

One more shrub Rose must be recommended where a tall hardy bush is required. This is *Rosa multiflora*, the Japanese Rose. It grows eight feet or more high, the strong canes set with huge bunches of small white flowers appearing more like Blackberry blossoms than like true Roses. These are followed by showy red fruits.

This is very little to say about a subject that is as wide as three continents. Numerous delightful native western species have not been mentioned, and persons who dwell in gentle climates will not fail to want to grow the lovely Cherokee Rose, *R. laevigata*, that is naturalized in many parts of the South. One of my best adventures had to do with keeping this tender Chinese Rose alive through three bitter winters in my Rockland County garden, and enjoying its wide, snowy, fragrant flowers against the south-facing wall. Nor would one having a suitable climate for it forgo the spectacular Macartney Rose, *R. bracteata*, white and shimmering, nor the dainty Banksias, white or yellow, double or single, in many-flowered umbels with a fragile scent.

In "Adventures in a Suburban Garden" there is a chapter devoted to old-fashioned Roses. These, as I therein pointed out, also make charming bushes for use along the foreground of shrubberies or in the flower borders among such old-time perennials as Sweet William, Foxgloves, Peonies, and old purple Iris.

And this seems a good place to tell of the work of two women, Mrs. Frank Lyon and Mrs. Frederick L. Keays, who at Lusby in Calvert County, Maryland, are engaged in an adventure that can have only the most delightful results for all Rose lovers. These women are gathering together from old gardens and from wherever they can get news of them, old-fashioned Roses, identifying them and making them available to the public. To read their steadily expanding list is like going among old and true friends, like meeting again those we have loved and thought of as lost. This is beautiful and significant work and deserves to be crowned with success.

CHAPTER XIX

SAGES OF SORTS

THE Sages have a long and honorable garden past. The common Sage, *Salvia officinalis,* that decks the sunny slopes above the Mediterranean with soft gray leaves and a haze of purple flower spikes, has been grown in English gardens since 1597, and it is one of the few herbs, popular in olden times, that are still in general use. "How can a man die who grows Sage in his garden?" was an old saying, and John Evelyn in his "Acetaria" thus sums up a list of its virtues: "In short 'tis a Plant endu'd with so many wonderful Properties, as that the assiduous use of it is said to render Men *immortal*: We cannot therefore but allow the tender *Summites* of the young leaves: but principally the *Flowers* in our cold Sallet; yet so as not to domineer."

Today we should not relish the rank tang of Sage in our salad, nor do we fancy the bitter Sage cheese that was once so popular. The decoctions of Sage leaves that were regarded by our foremothers as unfailing cure-alls, no longer are believed in, but the interior furnishings of goose and duck are dependent still for their zest upon a bit of this pungent herb—"yet so as not to domineer"—and if any herb at all is grown in modern gardens it is apt to be this one. Often in a

[166]

sunny corner of a vegetable garden a specimen or two of this comely old plant is to be found, and I know of one garden where it is used at the top of a retaining wall with fine effect, holding its own admirably with more newfangled decorations. Sage is quite easily raised from seed; any one wishing to add a bit of quiet but charming color to sunny borders for a small expenditure may do so by purchasing a packet of the seed of common garden Sage; he will find it listed among the Herbs in the vegetable section of catalogues.

The botanical name Salvia is from the Latin *salvere*, to be saved, and it was as agents of healing that the Salvias first came into gardens. Clary, or Clear-eyes, was an established inhabitant of the herb plot at an even earlier date than the common Sage. An infusion of its soft bitter leaves was a famous eye remedy, and when young and tender they were often chopped in an omelet or used as a garnish for salads. Clary wine was a much-liked beverage. Today Clary, *Salvia Sclarea,* has no uses at all other than ornamental, but it is really a beautiful plant, growing four feet tall, with large gray velvety leaves and cloudlike masses of pale or deep mauve bloom in summer. The individual blossoms are lavender, but they are set in conspicuous bracts of a pinkish tone which in combination with the gray leaves produce a most beautiful effect. Clary is a biennial, so must be raised from seed frequently, though it seeds itself rather freely in most gardens. Among the seedlings will be noted considerable variation in color tone, some being more desirable than others; but by careful selection it is easy enough to establish a good strain in your garden.

What Happens in My Garden

Clary blooms at the same time as does the glowing *Lilium Hansoni*, and the two are uncommonly handsome grown together. It was so that I first made their acquaintance, a great breadth of them, mingling their blossoms, so well set off by the velvet foliage of the Clary, in a famous Tuxedo garden. There is a handsome form of Clary—perhaps it is a distinct species, but it is much like, called *Salvia turkestanica*, that is pinker in effect than the ordinary Clary, and has the merit of remaining in bloom a very long time. Both are easily raised from seed, and both self-sow with a good deal of freedom.

The Salvias offer a great deal of real beauty and interest to the summer and autumn garden. Among them are annuals, biennials, hardy and half-hardy perennials, as well as some tender species of a sub-shrubby nature for use under glass. They contribute rich color and much diversity of form to the borders, and they are easily grown from seed or cuttings, and ask no more than commonly good soil and a sunny situation.

To begin with the annuals, every one knows and either adores or loathes (few are merely indifferent to it) the Scarlet Sage, *S. splendens,* in its several forms. Personally I feel that few gardens are large enough to hold the conflagration of this popular plant; the color is sharp and insistent, and it is not a flash of a moment for which we might be grateful, or at least tolerant —it goes on the summer through and well into the autumn, unflinching and undimmed. Too much of a good thing altogether.

Much better, though still rather sharp as to quality

is the new form of *Salvia splendens* called Salmon
Beauty. I saw it first in the Cambridge Botanic Garden
some years ago. It is a striking plant and, used with
restraint and companioned by white and lavender
flowers, will prove extremely valuable. There is also a
variety called Parma Violet which I have not seen, but
which is said to be a fine violet-blue. If it is as good as
report claims, it should be a real find, for this hue is
none too plentiful among flowers and is always valuable in the garden color scheme.

For many years I grew in my garden an annual Salvia called Blue Beard. It is a form of *S. Horminum,*
an old-fashioned species sometimes called Red Top or
Purple Top. The flowers of Salvia Blue Beard are
rather insignificant taken by themselves; the beauty
of the plant lies in the rich blue-purple hue of the bracts
which adorn the long stem for a length of perhaps eight
inches. They begin to color as they mature about midsummer and continue well into frosty weather, seeming to deepen in tone as the season advances. It is a
unique and most interesting annual and, massed near
the front of the borders behind buff-colored *Phlox
Drummondii* or some other becoming annual, is really
fine in effect. Blue Beard is a hardy annual and may
be sown early where the plants are to flower, or started
under glass if so desired. It self-sows freely and is good
for cutting.

Salvia patens is the half-hardy perennial whose vel-
vet-textured flowers are among the few that repeat the
rare hue of the Gentian at its best. It is used in this
part of the world chiefly as a bedding plant, being grown
under glass until wanted outside. It is a native of Mex-

ico. I cannot say that I have ever been especially successful in growing *Salvia patens,* but my equipment for starting things under glass is of the most sketchy. I understand that the roots of *Salvia patens* may be lifted in the autumn and stored like Dahlias. "The following spring these, when growth begins, may be increased by rooting the young shoots, placing them in a close frame where they quickly root, making good plants by the end of May."

The perennial Salvias are many and valuable, especially valuable because they are summer- and autumn-blooming, at which seasons their slender spiry habit and soft colors are exceedingly grateful to the eye. The Meadow Sage, *S. pratensis,* is a good early-blooming species with blue, rose, or white flowers in narrow spikes two and a half feet tall and a tidy habit. It is rather an old-fashioned plant apt to be neglected nowadays, but is important because it blooms for a long time in late June and July. If you raise it from seed there will be some choice among the seedlings as to color; some will be finer than others. The finest blue form is *S. p. Tenorii,* and it is worth taking a little trouble to secure it. The blossoms are fine dark blue. The Meadow Sages soon make generous wide clumps which should be divided every few years.

Salvia argentea, known as Silver Clary, is reliably perennial only on light soils and in sunny situations, and is best treated as a biennial; it is apt to die off after blossoming once. Its large tufts of silvery leaves are its chief attraction, as the pinkish white flowers are of small value. This plant is much used abroad for the sake of its foliage. *S. farinacea* is said to be a hardy perennial, but I have found it extremely short-lived. It is not a showy species; but the whole plant is delicately hoary, the flowers blue, and it makes an attractive feature in the borders grown with pink or violet flowers.

One of the best hardy herbaceous plants I know is *S. virgata nemorosa*. It grows neatly and bushily to a height of two feet, and in July and August presents a glowing mass of color. Dark blue flowers in crowded spikes terminate each stem, and they are set in reddish purple calyces which add a great deal to the richness of effect. They remain in perfection a long time. This fine plant is curiously neglected in America; it is not often offered by American dealers, which is a pity for it is a first-class plant. The white-flowered form is more often offered, but it is a poor thing not worth growing.

The lovely sky-blue color of certain of the Salvias is among the greatest blessings conferred upon the garden by this versatile family. The long cerulean flower spikes of *Salvia azurea* are known to most gardens. They are among the comparatively few true sky-blue flowers. If this plant has a fault it is that its stem is so slender that staking is necessary; and the habit of the plant causes it to be rather difficult to stake in an unobtrusive manner. Under no circumstances should the branches be tied tightly to a single stake. Bushy pea-brush inserted in front of the clump so that the stems may lean into it and so be upheld in a natural-looking way is the most satisfactory method, and some broad-beamed plant like a Phlox of medium height or Zinnias may be used to hide the pea-brush. Finer, a good deal, than *S. azurea,* however, and blooming longer and later, is *S. Pitcheri.* I think this used to be offered as *S. a. grandiflora,* and may still be in some catalogues. This is a truly grand hardy plant. The flowers are larger and of a deeper blue than those of *azurea,* and the plant is of sturdier port and more branching habit. It grows about four feet high, and the gentian-blue blossoms carried for a considerable length along the down-covered stems, are borne in September and October. Lovely combinations may be made with this plant and some of the pink-flowered hardy Asters, such as Peggy Ballard or Lady Lloyd, or with lemon-colored African Marigolds, or pink Zinnias, or yellow Gladioli, and it is delightful for cutting. *S. uliginosa* used once to be offered in most catalogues of hardy plants in this country. It is a sturdy branching plant, taller than either of the foregoing, and, though so slender in appearance, strong enough to stand without staking. This species grows about five feet high and forms clumps that may be three feet through. From the ends of all the leading shoots long panicles of sky-blue flowers appear in the late summer, followed shortly by many branching side shoots which continue the blossoming and give a fine bushy effect. I did not find this plant absolutely hardy in my cold Rockland County garden. Now and again a specially bitter winter took it off, and I had to begin all over again with it.

This fine plant seems to have disappeared from cata-logues, but it is listed in Dr. Bailey's "Hortus," so may still be somewhere about. Dr. Bailey calls it Bog Salvia and says it is a native of Brazil, Argentina, and Uru-guay. *S. azurea* is native of our southern states. We are proud to claim *S. Pitcheri* also as a compatriot. Its range is westward, from Minnesota and Illinois to Kansas, south to Texas.

Salvia glutinosa is a bold-growing yellow-flowered Sage native in parts of Europe and Asia. It grows three feet tall and has long racemes of pale yellow flowers in summer. I have seen it grown with interesting effect in front of a pale blue form of *Campanula lactiflora*. It is an uncommon species, but seed of it is to be had; and it is quite hardy.

South of Philadelphia the handsome red-flowered *S. Greggii* will stand over the winter out of doors. It is a very beautiful autumn-flowering species from Texas and Mexico, growing bushily to a height of two feet and bearing a profusion of bright carmine flowers over a long period. It is the hardiest of the shrubby Salvias. There is a white form of it that is less effective. Another handsome tender species is *S. Grahami,* with woody stems and masses of small bright crimson flowers, very nice for cutting. *S. rutilans* is an old greenhouse plant the leaves of which when touched give off the fragrance of pineapple.

S. involucrata (*S. Bethelli*) is another tender Salvia of great beauty, with large rose-colored flowers borne in autumn and large heart-shaped leaves veined with deeper color. All these tender Salvias and many more are conspicuous in the gardens of southern France and Italy during the winter months, and persons dwelling in the milder sections of our country would do well to make use of them, as their blossoming season is long and they are uncommon and interesting in effect.

CHAPTER XX

THE summer garden, like those who tend it through the long hot days, needs a stiffening, an astringent influence. Growth is soft and luxuriant, color riotous, unstinted. Plants that cool the whole show down and bind its parts together come as a distinct relief. "Plenty of white flowers," that too frequently offered palliative for the garden gone color-wild, do not turn the trick. On the contrary they merely break up the straining hues into hard units; they do not bring about unity. Plants with silvery or blue-green foliage and masses of gray-blue flowers make the best binders, and I have in mind the so-called garden Thistles with their severe, upright habit, and the metallic tones of both leaves and flowers as supplying that something austere and styptic which this season of laxness and lushness seems to stand in need of.

Perhaps to many reading this the very words "garden" and "Thistle" will seem violently inimical to each other. Few persons indeed would want the common wild Thistles loosed among their cherished borders. Most of us have suffered from them either as cultivators of the soil or as wayfarers because of their determined spread among crops or their prickly contact. But even these, the great Pasture Thistle with its honey-sweet balls of magenta bloom, and the little pestiferous Canada Thistle, if looked upon in their proper setting and without the memory of past injury, have real beauty for the seeing eye. Neither of these, by the way, though spread widely over our hospitable land, is what Mr. Bernard Shaw holds up to ridicule as a "hundred per cent American"; both came to us, as do many aliens, with assurance and insensitiveness in a high state of development.

But the Thistles under present consideration are not of these. Garden Thistles, so called, are of many kinds, but there is not space here to treat of them all. These notes are intended to serve merely as a finger pointing toward a closer acquaintance with a group of useful plants that is rather commonly neglected. They belong to three tribes, the Eryngiums, or Sea Hollies, members of the order Umbelliferae; the Echinops, or Globe Thistles; and the Carlinas, of the order Compositae. All are readily raised from seed, so that the fact that American nurserymen stock very few kinds is easily overcome. Some indeed, once established, look to their own seed-sowing sometimes in rather too free a manner, but the seedlings are distinct in appearance and easily detected and rooted out before they are too firmly anchored. They do not, as is the case with many a seedling wolf, appear garbed in the clothing of some innocent lamb until so firmly established that they are difficult to eradicate. They are quite hardy, especially if grown in light soil that has been deeply stirred, and full sun, the perennial species long enduring and not requiring frequent division; indeed they resent disturbance and are best left to form fine broad clumps, which they do without haste; the biennials of course die away after they have flowered, but leave a sufficient number of young about to take their places.

As being the finest and most useful among these Thistle-like plants we shall do well to consider first the Eryngiums, or Sea Hollies. The color of the stems of these plants, the spiny bracts, and the long teasel-like flower-heads, is silvery or blue of a distinctly metallic quality. They are for the most part deep-rooting hardy perennials, but one biennial species is exceedingly fine. They flower in July, and the silvery stems with their finishing clusters of blue "Thistles" may be made effective use of indoors.

Eryngium alpinum, the Sea Holly of Alpine pastures, is a most effective plant, the blue flowers surrounded by a double frill of shimmering silver bracts. The height is usually not more than eighteen inches, and in poor soil is sometimes less. With me, however, it has proved of biennial duration so must be raised from seed annually if it is to be maintained in the garden. Seed is offered in a number of catalogues, and the plants are not difficult to grow. It belongs to western and southern Switzerland, Jura, and Carinthia. Of a like dwarf stature is *E. Bourgati,* from stony pastures in the Pyrenees. A number of years ago I raised this species from seed, and I have enjoyed ever since its steadily widening stocky clumps as a foreground planting in sunny borders. It is a first-class hardy perennial. The effect of the plant is very blue, always with the characteristic metallic sheen. *E. Spinalba* is another dwarf and really lovely kind, seeds of which are to be had. It comes from Dauphiné, and the flower-heads are almost white as are the stem and the spiny frill.

Some years ago I saw in the rock garden at Kew a curious little Eryngium said to come from high up in the Sierra Nevada of Spain. This was *E. glaciale*. The plant was only about three or four inches high, the leaves extraordinarily spiny and silvery, and the little flower heads a pale metallic blue. I am unable to find this minute Sea Holly listed in any catalogue and should like well to know where seeds of it may be found. Mr. Farrer refers to *E. glaciale* as "the neatest, finest and most unfriendly of little thorny tuffets, armed in copious spikes of silvery grey, deepening towards shades of blue, with fishbone spines of ivory glinting as its stems of three or four inches unfold towards the frill and the flower." Mr. Farrer speaks also of *E. prostratum*, that "forms quite a small central rosette of thin oblong green leaves, sparingly toothed and wholly unarmed, from which lie out upon the earth in a star all round short prostrate stems of three or four inches, with flowers and frills of a beautiful blue." This, states Mr. Farrer, is a bog plant from Texas, and in damp places should make a running carpet, rooting as it goes, along all its ground-hugging branches. This plant is suspected of tenderness, even of being a biennial, but surely if it is of our own we should be able to secure it. I'd be glad if any reader would let me know where it may be found.

All the foregoing Eryngiums are suitable for the rock garden, the first three, of course, for a fairly spacious one, or they may be used in the foreground of borders. The last two are too small for any situation save the restricted one of a rock garden.

What Happens in My Garden

Bluest of the taller kinds and perhaps best is *E. Oli-verianum,* sometimes confused in nurseries with a rarer and inferior species, *E. amethystinum.* It grows about three feet tall, and after a few years forms fine permanent clumps, sending up many glistening silver-green stems branching into a fine cluster of flowers. Grown with the fragrant white Musk Mallow, *Malva moschata alba,* it makes a charming picture that lasts many weeks in good condition. *E. planum* is slenderer and not quite so tall, and the flowers are paler blue; but the plant is well branched and thrifty, and will flourish and endure in somewhat heavier soil than Sea Hollies in general.

Extraordinarily distinct and effective as a border plant is *Eryngium giganteum,* the Ivory Thistle, a biennial species from the Caucasian Alps and Armenia. This plant grows vigorously from three to four feet tall. The flowers are pale silvery blue, and are surrounded by a most spectacular frill of ivory-pale bracts which, according to Mr. Farrer, shine out so "ghostly clear" as to cause the plant to be known in its native habitat as Elves' Bones. Pink Hollyhocks make a fine background for the Ivory Thistle with clumps of Lyme Grass, *Elymus glaucus,* or the gray-leaved Funkias (Hostas), *F. Fortunei* or *F. Sieboldiana,* in the foreground, with groups of tall pink Snapdragons.

Gladioli in pink tones, or pale yellow, make a fine interplanting for clumps of Sea Hollies, and the feathery yellow-flowered Meadow Rue, *Thalictrum glaucum,* makes a good background for them, though the bloom of the Thalictrums will have almost gone when the Sea Hollies show best color.

Likely Thistles

The Globe Thistles, or Echinops, bloom somewhat later than the Sea Hollies; it might be said that they belong to August while the latter roughly belong to July. They are altogether of a bolder habit, somewhat taller, with Thistle-like leaves, gray or dusty-looking, and the flowers borne on stiff stems are gathered into perfectly round balls or a "globular cluster all resting on a common receptacle." The handsomest kind is probably *E. bannaticus* (*E. ruthenicus*) from Russia. This at its best is four feet tall, the effect of the whole plant silvery, the balls of bloom distinctly blue. It makes a bold and handsome companion for the summer Phloxes, Veronicas, Aconites, Helianthuses, Zinnias, and Marigolds of the last month of summer, and keeps its port and circumstance for a long time. Very good also are *E. Ritro,* called the Small Globe Thistle, growing three or four feet tall, with handsome pinnatifid leaves, downy on the undersides, and blue flowers; and a somewhat dwarfer kind, *E. humilis,* from the Caucasus. This has the characteristic Thistle-like foliage and balls of blue bloom, but grown on poor sandy soil the height is not more than two feet. All these are handsome and easily grown hardy perennials, thriving in ordinary light soil and full sun and increased readily by division of the clumps, by root cuttings, or by means of seed.

A striking biennial Globe Thistle is *Echinops sphaerocephalus,* especially the form known as *albidus,* which I have always called the Giant Silver Thistle, for the plant throughout—leaves, stems, and round flowerheads—is a pale silvery green, at times almost white. It is a giant indeed, towering magnificently at the back of the border, often to a height of seven feet, and gleaming in the sunshine. This biennial Thistle has a drawback in that it sows its hardy seed with an eagerness and determination that almost defies our utmost efforts to keep it in check. The stripling Thistles appear everywhere, in the most likely as well as the most unlikely situations, and rooting them out becomes a task to be carried out with swiftness and dispatch if one is to have a garden at all and not merely a patch of Thistles. Of course cutting off the flowering heads before seed has had time to mature is a certain defense against its wanton fecundity. Even then a few will escape our pains, and it is not likely that we shall ever be without a few representatives of this really handsome ornament, once we have admitted it to the garden.

Carlina ("from Carolinus, pertaining to Charles, commemorative of the famous Charlemagne, whose army was said to have been cured of the plague by it") is also well worth including in our family of garden-wise Thistles. *Carlina acanthifolia* is a biennial plant of great interest and striking effect. I grew it some years ago, and when it disappeared after the first flowering I, not knowing of its biennial habit, discarded it from mind as too uncertain. Now I know better, and a packet of seed recently sent me by Mr. Cleveland Morgan from his famous gardens in Montreal enables me to try again. This is the Stemless Thistle of the Alps, "where over the dry green slopes you may see outspread upon the ground its glittering star of intensely spiny handsome leaves, while in the middle sits flat upon it an immense Everlasting-flower, suggesting some wild water-lily invented for an evil sea by Aubrey Beardsley, shimmering, silvery and immortal." Farrar, of course.

Likely Thistles

This unusual plant is exceedingly effective in a bold position in the rock garden, where there is space for its generous spread. In order to keep its great rosette flat and its blossoms stemless, the soil it grows in must be poor, half starved, and perfectly drained, as well as open to the brightest sun.

Carlina acaulis is interesting, too, and though low-growing is not, as the name untruthfully implies, a stemless species. It, too, is properly housed on a large rock garden in full sun. The white suns of flowers are borne on very short stems against a mass of silvery spiny leaves. "It thrives in a deep light soil, especially in limestone, and in very sunny situations." *C. acaulis* is a hardy perennial and does not, like *C. acanthifolia,* die after blossoming.

CHAPTER XXI

A VICTORIAN FAMILY—THE FUNKIAS (HOSTAS)

THE Funkias, or Plantain Lilies, as they are called because of their broad ribbed foliage, are as Victorian as antimacassars or chaperons; but there is about them a certain dignity and civility often characteristic of the properties of the Victorian Age which recommends them to our less stable and more restless day. There is certainly nothing flighty or ephemeral about the Plantain Lilies—nothing very exciting, either, it may be argued; but their usefulness in the garden is nevertheless definite and authentic. They have an advantage over many a more spectacular plant family in that they settle down, without fuss or unreasonable demands, to long-tenure residence in one situation, and are permanently and increasingly ornamental. Any plant that has foliage of such lasting good quality is of real importance to the border gardener who tries to keep a best foot foremost throughout the season. And it is in this case especially that the Funkias get in their good work.

Probably most of us are accustomed to thinking of these plants as very old-fashioned—they have a quaint simplicity which seems not of this day—but as a matter of fact they were all, save *Funkia ovata* (*F. caerulea*), which came into cultivation at the end of the eighteenth century, introduced to gardens during the nineteenth century. They enjoyed an immediate vogue in that day when simple rather stately things were well thought of, and there was scarce a garden that did not boast a round or oval bed upon the lawn filled with one or other of the Plantain Lilies, while the curse was lifted from many a dank stretch of shrubbery by a banding of their rich persistent green. Today we do better by them. We have learned more of their possibilities and versatility, and lozenge beds upon the greensward are happily no longer permissible. For massing in the indeterminate region between lawn and woodland any of the kin are excellent, or for shrouding the nether limbs of shrubs. By the waterside they have a special appropriateness of appearance, and they thrive in the dampish soil. In the borders their broad handsome foliage and prodigally borne spikes of bell-like pendent flowers, white or in various tones of lavender to deep blue-violet, lend an effect of restrained gaiety and stability. Especially are they valuable for corner and angle planting, where a lasting display of good foliage is imperative, and their definitely spreading and substantial character makes them particularly happy for use in combination with slender spiry types of plants.

So far as their blossoming goes, they are plants of the summer, the different kinds covering a period of from June until September. They belong to the Lily order and have thick durable roots that gradually form large symmetrical clumps. They thrive best in rich, deep, and moisture-retentive soil, not necessarily damp; and if the soil is on the heavy side they are perfectly comfortable in full sun; in thinner, more shallow soil there should be shade for at least part of the day. But they are in no way demanding and will endure surprisingly under most indifferent conditions. Autumn is a good time to set out the Plantain Lilies, though spring will do, and they are easily increased by cutting up the clumps with a sharp knife. Several crowns should be left to each new clump. If Funkias have a fault, it is that the foliage is rather deliberate about putting in an appearance in the spring. But during the many weeks between their rising and their setting they give a good account of themselves. The plants are very long-lived and need not be divided for years on end if they are blossoming satisfactorily; but they suffer in times of drought and should be watered freely if the best results with them are to be obtained.

There are, according to the Kew Hand-List, seven species of Funkia, all native in Japan, and most of these have several varieties. The species run easily to variegations; and forms with the leaves edged, striped, or marbled with yellowish white are common and not especially desirable, though in rural neighborhoods and in old gardens they were, and still are, popular for edging beds and paths.

The earliest kind to bloom, and the oldest in gardens, is *Funkia ovata*. It flowers, according to locality, in late June or early July, and it is distinguished by striking foliage, dark green and heart-shaped, and racemes of pretty pendent "lilies," lilac, or paler, and about fifteen to a stem carried a foot and a half above the spreading leaves. It is good massed at the turn of a border with the cloudy haze of *Gypsophila paniculata* behind it, out of which may arise effectively the yellow-flowered spikes of *Thermopsis montana* planted just beyond.

Funkia lancifolia blooms in August, the flowers carried on slender stems but very little above the narrow leaves. This species has many forms; one of them, *F. tardiflora*, is the latest of the Plantain Lilies to bloom. There is a very pretty white-flowered form of *lancifolia* also, and several with the characteristic yellowish markings on the leaves. In August, amidst the gay motley of that lavish month, these cool-flowered Funkias are very welcome and combine happily with the later-flowering Phloxes, Marigolds, Calendulas, and the like. *F. lancifolia* is the most profuse-flowering of all the species, and makes a pleasant foreground planting for masses of *Lilium speciosum*, either the pink or the white form.

The best known of the Funkias is the old Corfu Lily, or White Day Lily, *Funkia subcordata*, and it is often the most sinned against in the matter of situation, being too frequently consigned to hopelessly unsanitary locations beneath the shade of heavy branches or in dry sun-parched borders. It is worthy of a better fate, for it is a handsome plant; the broad leaves are a refreshing lettuce-green in color, and the frosted white "lilies" carried well above the foliage are deliciously fragrant. They appear in August and continue often into September. The White Day Lily responds generously to generous treatment, loving sunshine and a rich, deep, well manured soil. I once saw in a lovely old Salem garden a long straight path leading from the doorway of the white colonial house to the gate, bordered on either side with white Corfu Lilies and single white Petunias. The effect was reserved and quaintly charming by day as befitted this stately old home; but by night it had a quite eerie loveliness, and one's senses were drowned in perfumes that were the reverse of reserved or restrained.

Two species of Plantain Lilies are important to the gardener by reason of the attractive glaucous tones of the leaves. These are *F. Sieboldiana* and *F. Fortunei*. The first-named is perhaps the finest of all the Funkias for foliage, and it blooms somewhat earlier than *F. Fortunei*. The leaves are very large and broad and beautiful both in their modeling and in the unusual bluish caste of color. It may be used as a special feature in any ornamental planting of large scale such as in broad groups at the edge of woodland or in bays in the shrubbery. The blossoms are a lovely creamy-lilac color and hang in a graceful one-sided spike.

The leaves of *F. Fortunei* are somewhat smaller; but it too when established is a vigorous species, and the steel-blue of the leaves is very pronounced. Being somewhat less tropical in appearance, this species is better than the foregoing for general border planting. It makes a delightful foreground planting for groups of Musk Mallows, *Malva moschata*, especially the mauve kind, or for *Physostegia virginica* in its improved form, *P. v. grandiflora*, the color of which is deeper than that of the Musk Mallows.

I have in my rock garden a very dwarf Plantain Lily that I am unable to identify. It came to me as *Funkia minor*, but this name is nowhere listed that I can find. It blooms in August with the Corfu Lily and, though infinitely smaller in all its parts, resembles this old favorite. The leaves are rather narrow, and it is rather grudging in increase, never forming a very generous clump; but it is valuable in the rock garden because the pretty white flowers come at a season when there is little in bloom in that region. It is quite possible that my *Funkia minor* is one of the numerous forms of the variable *F. lancifolia*.

One hears sometimes of *F. glauca* and of *F. longipes*, but I have seen neither of them in the flesh. The first is said to be very attractive, with bluish leaves and lavender flowers on stems a foot above the foliage.

I am told that the Funkias make handsome pot or tub plants in windows and conservatories as well as out of doors on terraces. Miss Jekyll especially recommends *F. Fortunei* for the latter purpose. In shaded places the Funkias combine well with Ferns, with the white Turtlehead and with the easily grown Bottle Gentian, *Gentiana Andrewsii*.

CHAPTER XXII

THE POMP OF THE MULLEINS

CERTAIN plant families are conspicuously and unaccountably neglected by American gardeners, amateur and professional. In the forefront of these are the Mulleins, or Verbascums. Perhaps the reasons are not far to seek. As gardeners many of us have not yet begun to cultivate that power to take pains that is the part of a good gardener no less than that of genius. And Mulleins, though they are so easy to grow, do nevertheless cause us some trouble because most of them are biennial by nature, and even those designated as perennial are short-lived unless grown in light, poorish soil, well drained and in fullest sun.

We do like, the majority of us, to see the same dear flowers lift up the same dear faces (if some liberty may be taken with the poet) in the selfsame places year after year, with as little trouble as possible to ourselves; and we are continually left in the lurch by Mulleins if we have not been so forehanded as to keep a supply coming on in seed beds to take the places of the departed, as we are accustomed to doing with Foxgloves and Canterbury Bells. We are resigned to the behavior of these two famous biennials, but we have not yet got round to putting up with like idiosyncrasies in Mulleins. Nurserymen in particular have no patience with such unstable wares though I know one (more power to him) who lists five of the best kinds in his catalogue, and I shall be glad to give his name to any one who will write and ask me for it.

Moreover, we are afraid of that word "weed," and the name Mullein in the minds of many of us is synonymous with this outlaw term. Weeds, it might be said, are Nature's sins of commission, and we as a nation are pledged to blot out sins—of commission rather than omission. Hence we do not countenance weeds. But if any one with an eye for line and color can view without interest a raw roadside cut rescued from blatant hideousness by the intervention of the amazing dignity and beauty of crowding, towering stalks of what we are pleased to call our native Mullein (*Verbascum Thapsus*), it is difficult to think that he himself is not a sin of commission on the part of improvident Providence.

But to begin at the beginning: The name Verbascum is an old Latin one that I read was originally Barbascum, meaning bearded, because of the bearded stamens. The origin of the common name Mullein I do not know for certain, but it is very old. Early writers spelled it variously Moleyne, Molleyne, Mollen, Mullen; Lyte gives Wolleyn or Wulleyn, and as Gerard says "Mullein or rather Woolen," it seems these names all derive from the characteristic woolliness which marks most of the species.

Mulleins inhabit Europe, North Africa, and western and central Asia—America only by adoption. We have no native Mulleins despite the prevalence all across our country, north and south, of *Verbascum Thapsus, V.*

Blattaria, the pretty little Moth Mullein, and others. Not all are suitable for garden decoration, though I never saw any that lacked a decided decorative quality such as is possessed by *Thapsus* of the scarred roadsides. Garden plants are required to hit you in the eye, so to speak, before they are admissible, and *V. Thapsus* has a stingy way of opening its blossoms one by one, or a few at a time; and so this plant so aptly called Hightaper is not deemed fit for garden circles. So, too, the Moth Mullein, *V. Blattaria,* for all its quaint charm of slender stalk set with round yellow or white blossoms, is a bit too wayward, too noncomforming to garden standards, though a pleasant enough companion when one is on the loose, so to speak, having escaped from trim garden ways to the freedom of the countryside with the "key of the fields" in one's pocket.

But for the strictly garden-minded there are plenty of Mulleins, though of all of them it must be said that they have the look of things but once removed from the wild, not untidy, not gauche, but affinitive certainly with free spirits. In England a race of hybrid Mulleins in beautiful and unusual colors has been developed, but that we may not have them goes without saying, so we need not dwell here on the tones of cinnabar-red, of buff-terra-cotta, of bronzy yellow that they display, but had better turn our attention to what is still within our reach.

Mulleins are essentially of the summer months, and for the most part they grow tall—from five to eight feet. In these two respects they are extremely valuable to the gardener. The inflorescence is either in a long spike like a candle, or in the form of a candelabra, with many branching arms; and the color most commonly displayed further carries out the analogy to light, for it is yellow, a yellow of a peculiarly radiant quality. The first time I ever saw Mulleins used in a garden was in England more than twenty years ago, in a little lane with sloping sides that connected two sections of a large garden. *Verbascum olympicum* with its enormous candelabras was planted thickly along the sloping sides of the lane, and though the day was overcast and dusk approaching, the tens of thousands of little yellow blossoms gave a very fair counterfeit of a gala illumination.

Mulleins are valuable in the garden not only because of their height and their color (which seems to blend with all other colors happily), but because they have a very long period of blossoming during summer, and because even when the blossoming period is past the tall gray stalks possess a comely dignity that causes us to let them stand. The plants, if allowed to mature their seed, self-sow freely so that there are always plenty of gray velvet rosettes to be taken up in the spring and transplanted to situations where we would have them. These plants are eminently fit for border use, for planting in bays in the shrubbery, for groups in the wild garden; and one or two are even suitable for the rock garden. For the best effect they should always be planted in groups, and they are so easy to grow from seed that any one who can achieve Zinnias and Marigolds and Hollyhocks may have Mulleins. They have also the good quality of being drought-resistant, standing up manfully beneath our hottest suns.

When we come to consider the kinds I must begin with my first love—*Verbascum olympicum*, the Olympic Mullein, which I still think the handsomest and most valuable of all the kinds I have grown. In my experience it is not a biennial but a triennial, for it takes three years from seed to mature its immense flowering stalk. This sounds a lengthy business, but after the first wait, which does require patience, there will always be plenty of seedlings for use where they are required. It is a noble and stately plant, quite architectural in the ordered arrangement of its tiers of long rough leaves that clasp and hide the stem for half its length and then give way before the aspiration of the blossoming column some thirty or forty inches long, interrupted at more or less regular intervals by the flowering branches that give it its candelabra look. The main flower stem and its branches, though set thickly with buds, do not give a crowded or disordered appearance, for the flowers do not open all at once but twinkle forth a few at a time over a period of three months or more. Think of the short and hurried blossoming of Foxgloves and Canterbury Bells, and the care which we must take to keep them in our midst, and then of this generous, splendid plant, defying drought, blossoming for months and perpetuating itself without any trouble on our part! I have seen its seedlings in some queer places, but never did they seem out of place: once in a flight of broad stone steps where they grew shorter than common because of lack of nourishment; once in a high dry wall where they reached toward heaven in a most gracious gesture; many times at a border edge where they should have appeared amiss but did not. I cannot pass on to the other kinds before I have recommended *Verbascum olympicum* as a cure for commonplaceness in any garden, and mentioned its curious pleasant fragrance.

V. phlomoides also has great claims to distinction. It is handsome from top to toe, from its great woolly rosette up its leafy stem to the tip of its long gold candlestick. The stalk has a few branches, and the flowers are the color of Evening Primrose, five-petaled and about an inch across. Its defect is that these flowers remain open only while the sun shines upon them, though even in cloudy weather the six- or seven-foot stalk seems a gray staff and has real decorative value.

V. pannosum (*V. longifolium*) is the giant of the family so far as height is concerned, reaching eight feet on occasion and in congenial surroundings. The very large and long leaves are silvery, the flower spike somewhat branched and well clothed with sulphur-yellow flowers. It comes from Macedonia.

Verbascum Chaixii is listed as a perennial, but with me has not proved long-lived. It was one of Miss Jekyll's favored plants, and she suggests placing it next to *Thalictrum flavum*. The tone of the Mullein's yellow is considerably deeper than that of the Meadow Rue and its dignified carriage complements well the spready, small-leaved habit of the latter. A few pale Delphiniums add to the attractiveness of this grouping. *V. Chaixii* is not as tall as many Mulleins but can usually be counted upon to reach a height of five feet. There is a white-flowered form, but I have not seen it. The white-flowered Mullein with which I am most familiar is the hybrid Miss Willmott. This, as I have proved many times, comes true from seed, which seems not to be the case with the other hybrids. It is a valuable plant, growing five feet or more in height, with woolly foliage and a long spike of creamy flowers produced over a long period at midsummer. A delightful grouping for midsummer enjoyment is composed of generous clumps of the purple Loosestrife, many stalks of Miss Willmott's Mullein, and in front of them a mass of the white Mullein Pink (*Agrostemma coronaria alba*) and some clumps of the shock-headed yellow Knapweed, *Centaurea macrocephala*. This planting keeps its beauty for several weeks, and even after the flowering is past the texture and tones of the foliage and the sustained good form of the taller plants make it a continued pleasure.

Another white-flowered Mullein which is worth growing is *V. nigrum album*. This is less tall and imposing than many of its cousins, but an admirable border plant nevertheless, three feet tall, with smooth leaves and an unbranched spike of white flowers enhanced by purple centers. It is superior to the yellow form and comes into bloom early in July.

Verbascum densiflorum (*V. thapsiforme*) I have found rather longer-lived though somewhat less effective than other Mulleins. It grows five feet tall, the whole plant densely covered with soft yellowish hairs. The flowers of the characteristic yellow hue string the long candlestick in little sessile clusters. It is a European species.

In a short chapter one cannot cover the subject of Mulleins with satisfactory adequacy, but before closing there is one more that must be mentioned. This is *V. phoeniceum*, which, instead of following the yellow tradition of its family, gives us round flowers of rose, pink, salmon, mauve, and purple, as well as white.

The Pomp of the Mulleins

The plants rarely exceed two feet in height, are bushy and freely branched, a fine subject for the foreground of borders or for the rock garden, where height is desired. This Mullein is listed as a perennial, but again its behavior in this part of the world does not always bear out this contention. Its flat self-sown rosettes are among the pleasant finds of spring, however. Once given encouragement, it will not fail you.

The seed of Mulleins, despite their towering size, is very small, and one must have a care to sow thinly and afterwards to thin out the seedlings to several inches apart, discarding or transplanting the thinnings. The seed bed should be in a warm, sunny situation, the soil well drained. They may be sown in early spring, and blossoming plants (save of *V. olympicum*) secured for next year's enjoyment. In gardens where a number of kinds are grown, the seedlings seldom come true, for the different species cross readily; but this only adds to the interest.

CHAPTER XXIII

THERE is so much to be said for Honeysuckles, and so much of it is pleasant, that one despairs of being able to compress it within the compass of a short chapter. In the first place it is a great race. The Kew Hand-List of Trees and Shrubs lists ninety-nine species, besides many varieties. Among them are both evergreen and deciduous kinds, some of climbing habit, others growing into graceful wide-spreading bushes. They are widely distributed in the northern hemisphere, and while certain species will not endure out of doors in the colder parts of the country, for the most part we may paraphrase the old nursery rhyme and say that when they are hardy they are very, very hardy. The Himalayan species are apt to be tender but a majority of the others are among the very best cold climate plants.

The family is the Caprifoliaceae, to which belong also the dainty Linnaea of our cold northern woods and the popular garden Weigela. The generic name, Lonicera, was bestowed in honor of a German botanist, one Adam Lonicer, who lived in the sixteenth century. The pretty common name explains itself and has long been in use though sometimes shared by other plants, among them the Red Clover and the pink wild Azalea, *A. nudiflora*. When early works on plants spoke of "Honeysuckle" or "Woodbynde," however, they had in mind a species of Lonicera.

The tubular flowers of Honeysuckles, while seldom showy, have a sprightly grace and are often borne with such riotous freedom, sometimes in the axils of the leaves, again in terminal bunches, as to make the bush or vine a conspicuous and charming object. Many of the species add delicious fragrance to their other attractions, and altogether it is rather astonishing that so few kinds are commonly grown. A garden of any size and pretension usually boasts many kinds of Lilacs, often a fine collection of Mock Oranges, even of Barberries and Cotoneasters; but the Honeysuckles, save for a few kinds, are conspicuously neglected. This is the more remarkable as they are not difficult of culture, any fair soil and situation sufficing for their needs. The climbing varieties for the most part are woodland plants and thrive best in cool leaf-moldy soil out of the hottest sun. The bush varieties, on the other hand, love sunshine and should stand free of other shrubs where they may develop their special grace without hindrance or crowding. I have found them easily moved at almost any season, even when in full leaf, if the bushes are kept watered after this major operation.

The charming flexuous climber which Turner in his "Names of Herbes" (1548) called Wod bynde is *Lonicera Periclymenum*. This is the plant that graces British hedgerows and scents the countryside. Gerarde wrote of it, "It groweth in woods and hedges and upon shrubbes and bushes, often times winding itselfe so straight and hard about that it leaveth his print upon these things so wrapped." In this country the Virginia

Creeper is often called Woodbine, and other climbers
that have borne the expressive name are the Ivy and the
Clematis. *Loricera Periclymenum* and its variety the
Dutch Honeysuckle, *L. belgica,* are highly desirable
climbers, bearing their pale tubular blossoms, streaked
on the outsides with carmine, in terminal bunches
throughout the summer and filling the air about with a
rare sweetness. They climb to a height of about twenty
feet. More commonly seen in this country is the variety
of *L. japonica,* known as Hall's Honeysuckle. This is
dense in habit, and the leaves persist almost throughout
the winter. It is a constant bloomer, the flowers opening
white and changing to a soft corn-color as they age,
and it is often possible to gather a sprig of the fragrant
flowers from a sheltered corner as late as Thanksgiving.
Another form of *L. japonica,* and one that is not as
popular as it deserves to be, is the pretty Golden Honeysuckle, *L. j. aureo-reticulata,* the leaves of which are
marbled with gold and the young growths often delicately tinted pink. It is a most cheerful drapery for
a dull corner and, where grown against a trellis or
balustrade, makes a good background for a border
planted with blue, mauve, yellow, and white flowers.

Our native Trumpet Honeysuckle, *L. sempervirens,*
scentless alas, is found from Connecticut to Florida and
Texas. It is a beautiful and conspicuous climber with
its bunches of scarlet, orange-lined tubes, showing so
handsomely against the bluish foliage. *L. Heckrottii,*
said to be allied to it, is different in that the flowers
are pinkish without and yellow within and are quite
fragrant at night. It is a very hardy and attractive
species. The southern Honeysuckle, *L. flava,* that grows

wild in woody places from North Carolina to Oklahoma, bears bright orange-colored fragrant flowers in the early summer. It is rarely seen but is a delightful species, evergreen, and quite hardy, at least as far north as New York City. There is a fine specimen in Herbert Durand's garden.

The great Chinese Woodbine, *L. tragophylla,* introduced by the late Mr. Wilson in 1900, is "distinguished among Honeysuckles by the size of its flowers which are borne in heads of ten to twenty blossoms of a uniform rich canary yellow." It is a handsome plant worthy a place among the choicest climbers and is hardy as far north as New England. It lacks only fragrance to make it a really great acquisition.

In southern gardens I have seen the lovely and exquisitely fragrant *L. etrusca,* sometimes called the Italian Woodbine. This is perhaps the most beautiful of its kind, flinging out bunches of bloom from the ends of the branches as well as from the axils of the leaves, the individual flowers being two inches long, at first yellowish suffused with red, but becoming clear yellow with age, and the foliage distinctly bluish in cast and downy on the undersides. *L. Hildebrandiana* too is a grand species for the South, the far South, southern California or Florida. It is an evergreen from Upper Burma, a vigorous, tall-growing climber hanging out splendid clusters of very long, slender tubular blossoms, purplish in the bud and opening to pale yellow.

Several European Honeysuckles have become naturalized in this country, among them *L. Caprifolium,* the Goat Honeysuckle, with tubular flowers, white or purplish, and exceedingly fragrant, borne in whorls and in pairs in the early summer and followed by orange fruit. It is seldom seen in gardens and, though a charming kind, has not a long blossoming period to recommend it.

Among the desirable bush Honeysuckles we must pick and choose, for they are many and space is limited. Many of them may be said to give two performances, for besides their flowers the majority of them also offer bright and conspicuous fruits. To begin with the earliest to flower, we have *L. Standishii* and *L. fragrantissima*. If I were restricted to an allowance of a half-dozen shrubs in my garden, one of these would, I am sure, be among them, not so much for the intrinsic beauty as for the rich fragrance emitted by the creamy, paired blossoms before the leaves appear that informs all the air for yards about them, in March. They may, if desired, be grown in a thicket of other shrubs whence they will send forth their greeting with the first relenting days. These shrubs are perhaps not so fine in form as others of their kin, but they are sub-evergreen, the grayish leaves lasting until Christmas in the neighborhood of New York. There is little difference between the two species, and they are commonly sent out impartially the one for the other from many nurseries.

Two other species noted for their fragrance are the Chinese *L. syringantha,* and its finer variety *Wolfii,* and *L. thibetica.* The first has a somewhat drooping habit and makes a twiggy wide-spreading shrub bearing in May, in axillary clusters, lavender heliotrope-scented blossoms, almost hidden among the grayish leaves. The blossoms are followed by red berries. *L. thibetica* is a good deal like it but is smaller in all its parts, and the leaves are covered on the undersides with a gray down or felt. *L. syringantha Wolfii* is to be preferred to either of these two because of its better form and richer-colored blossoms that look like little sprays of Lilac.

Lonicera Korolkowii is a recent introduction from Turkestan and is a shrub of most unusual beauty. It grows ultimately twelve feet high, and against the loose-spreading and arching branches clothed in blue-green leaves it showers out in late May or early June an enveloping spray of pink bloom. This fine shrub is perfectly hardy in New England and should be given plenty of room in which to spread its skirts and display its undoubted charm. Another very unusual species is *L. Ledebourii*, not nearly as tall as the foregoing and of a stiffish erect habit. The leaves are somewhat pubescent, giving the shrub a soft slurred appearance, and deep orange-yellow flowers tinged with red are borne in pairs in the leaf axils in early summer. These are followed so precipitately by shiny black berries set in rose-colored bracts that fruit and flowers are often found upon the bush at the same time. It is a native of California.

Of the older kinds very important are *L. Maacki, L. Morrowi, L. tatarica, and L. bella.* All these are strong growers, hardy and effective. The first, *L. Maacki*, grows in time to a height of fifteen feet, a tall upright shrub of spreading habit, deciduous, with broad shining leaves and masses of flowers sprigged all along the branches. These are white, changing to corn color as they age, with delicate carmine markings on the exterior. The succeeding dark red fruits hang long after the leaves have fallen, making it a decorative object in the late autumn garden. It is from Manchuria. *L. Morrowi* is a free-growing Japanese species not as tall as *L. Maacki,* but of good form and vigorous constitution. It reaches a height of eight feet and will be as broad as tall. The flowers are cream-white and sweet-scented, appearing in May and June, and are followed by gay scarlet berries, ripening at midsummer but remaining on the bushes until far into the autumn.

The Tatarian Honeysuckle, *L. tatarica,* is an old favorite with its erect habit and masses of pinkish drooping two-lipped flowers, borne in axillary pairs that do not, after the habit of so many Honeysuckle flowers, change to yellow as they age. This is a native of southern Russia and Siberia, and there are numerous forms, some better than others. The pretty and floriferous *L. bella* is a hybrid between the two foregoing species, *L. Morrowi,* and *L. tatarica,* and has inherited some of the best points of both. It grows rapidly into a wide-spreading bush from six to eight feet high, the foliage dusty gray, the flowers, like those of the Tatar parent, pinkish. In the variety *albida* the flowers are pure white. In this garden it self-sows freely, youngsters springing up all about it. It will grow happily and blossom almost anywhere, even on the north side of a building.

Two evergreen species that may be found exceedingly useful are *L. nitida* and *L. pileata. L. nitida,* the Box Honeysuckle, growing slowly to a height of six feet, is proving valuable as a hedge plant in certain parts of the country where the mercury does not fall too low. It is not hardy in New England. The leaves are small and shining, and the habit of the plant close and dense, which enables it to stand clipping to a formal line. The blossoms are creamy white, borne in pairs, and are fragrant. This is one of Mr. Wilson's valuable introductions from China. Young specimens of it are attractive in the rock garden, but a more suitable rock-garden kind is *L. pileata,* dwarf and spreading in habit, appearing much like a Cotoneaster, with small Box-like leaves shining and persistent of a rich deep green color. Half hidden among the leaves in spring are clusters of sweet-scented creamy trumpets, and later translucent purple fruit. Its home is in central China, and it is quite hardy in the neighborhood of New York.

This is little enough to say about so vast a subject, but many a less deserving plant finds its way into our gardens than these amiable and attractive Honeysuckles. When the next order for shrubs goes forth surely some of these should find a place thereon.

CHAPTER XXIV

CLEMATIS

Of all climbers sung by poets or acclaimed by gardeners none has the invariable and beguiling grace that distinguishes the members of the Clematis tribe. Whatever the type or whatever the position it is called to adorn, it takes its place with a charming ease, a wayward but delicate flexuousness that unfailingly charms the beholder. There is no situation, seemingly, in which it cannot make itself appear unstudied and perfectly at home.

Clematis is a great race belonging to the Buttercup order and widely distributed in the North Temperate Zone. It is a genus of deciduous climbing shrubs, mostly woody and herbaceous perennials, with a few evergreen species. The blossoming of the various kinds covers almost the whole growing season, from early spring through autumn, and the way they go to seed, flying their smoky feather-tailed seed vessels, is as attractive as their extravagant and lovely blossoming. Many give truly gorgeous displays of blossoms, and some possess a fine fragrance which they give off freely to the air. There are few garden situations where one or another of them may not be used to advantage. Let them climb a trellis or be trained against a wall; let them scramble over fences with climbing Roses, or over old tree stumps or low shrubs, let them surge riotously over rocky precipitous ground, or train them on posts at the back of herbaceous borders (the large-flowered kinds are the best for this purpose), and the effect they produce will always be highly gratifying.

And yet they are strangely absent from the majority of American gardens. The Japanese Virgin's Bower, *Clematis paniculata,* is found in most gardens, and occasionally a good piece of the lovely old *C. Jackmani,* with its splendid enveloping bloom, but certainly no general use is made of these beautiful climbers.

This scarcity of the Clematis in our gardens may possibly be due to the fact that attempts to grow any but the amiable Japanese Virgin's Bower have met with failure, and in our impatience other more amenable subjects have been chosen in its place. The fact is that these plants, the majority of them, have certain definite requirements that must be met; when these are understood and complied with, there is little trouble in growing any of the species, and even the superb large-flowered hybrids may be attempted with a very fair certainty of success.

The first of these requirements is probably a degree of lime in the soil. Any one who has seen their superb performance in the neighborhood of Bath, England, where the subsoil is chalk, will readily understand that lime contributes much to their well-being. Nevertheless, Mr. William Robinson, who has long made a specialty of Clematises in his garden in Sussex, maintains that although the Clematis is essentially a plant of calcareous regions, it will succeed in ordinary soil. "At Gravetye," he says, "when making fresh plantations, the soil, three feet deep, is made up of loam and leaf soil with a good proportion of sand. Nothing is added but a mulch of bracken. No manure is given."

Other authorities, on the other hand, strongly recommend the addition of lime in some form; and in certain parts of the United States where the soil is naturally acid, often very acid, this is undoubtedly a first necessity. The making up of the soil so that it will be loose and well drained is also important, and it has frequently been pointed out that the Clematis, for all its fragile appearance, has a good appetite and quickly exhausts the soil, so that a dressing of bonemeal or cow manure, well rotted, may well be added at the time of planting, and a mulch of nourishing material applied early in the spring, so that the young shoots will have something to feed upon in their early stages.

J. E. Spingarn, who at his estate Troutbeck, Amenia, New York, grows Clematis with conspicuous success, and who has made a careful study of the race and its needs, says, "Nearly all Clematis are lime-lovers, and the American species are no exception to the rule. When introducing a new species to the garden, it is nearly always safe to add a liberal quantity of ground limestone. I believe that lack of lime (or at the very best acidity of the soil) accounts for failure in growing Clematis more than perhaps any other single cause. For most of them, a compost consisting of loam, leaf mold, sand, and well-rotted manure, to which ground limestone has been added at the rate of one spadeful of limestone to a wheelbarrowful of soil, will provide an ideal home in which to grow; but if the soil is at all sour or acid, two or even more spadefuls may be added."

Clematis

The second requirement is undoubtedly some degree of shade. Clematises are, it must be remembered, naturally copse plants, or grow on the fringes of woods, twining up through bushes or climbing up the tree trunks, so that the stems for a considerable length are protected from drying influences, while the flowering growths fling themselves out into the sunshine. This is a lesson to be taken to heart. We must not get the idea, however, that these plants will thrive in dank situations, such as heavy woodland; but undoubtedly the stem should be protected for a portion of its length from the burning rays of the sun. Growing them through open shrubs such as Magnolias or Hawthorns gives this consoling shelter; or they may be trained up the west side of an Apple or Pear tree with beautiful effect, and the slender climber will do no harm whatever to its sturdy support.

It is with the beautiful large-flowered hybrids, of mixed and often obscure origin, that we experience the most trouble, and it is the burden of Mr. Robinson's cry that when we can secure these lovely things on their own roots, rather than grafted on wild and often unsuitable stock, our trouble with them will be largely over. They are, nevertheless, worth all the trouble and travail of spirit they cause, and in spite of their bad reputation often prove most unexpectedly long-lived and even tough.

There was an old vine of *Jackmani* with a great woody stem that grew on the porch of my old Rockland County home. It had been there for years and met every sort of vicissitude, from children swinging on it to being eaten to the ground by an omnivorous puppy, with an undimmed cloak of purple bloom that was almost startling in its gorgeousness. I suppose this old plant bore out Mr. Robinson's contention, for it was certainly not a grafted specimen. But in that garden, which had naturally much lime in the soil, throve also the beautiful *C. Henryi*, with its immense white blossoms, and on the Rose pergola a Clematis was planted beside each Rose and contended charmingly for a place in the sun. They throve satisfactorily and were long-lived.

The soil of my present garden is at once too heavy and too acid to be to the liking of the Clematis tribe, and I have not yet got around to contriving conditions that will meet the necessities of the large-flowered kinds. But the small-flowered species thrive easily, and many of them are very effective. Moreover they are easily raised from seed. A. J. Macself, in his invaluable book "Plants from Seed," has this to say about raising Clematises from seed:

"Put the fluffy seeds, as soon as gathered, into a box half filled with dry sand. Close the lid and shake well, to get the seed well distributed through the sand. Spread thinly and evenly over the bed and cover with a half-inch layer of sand and leafmold in equal proportions. Water well with a fine-rosed can, and shake a loose light covering of chaff over the bed. Germination will be slow (as it is with all the Buttercup tribe), but the chaff may be removed in spring, the bed again watered and kept moist throughout the summer. The following spring transplant the young roots."

There are numerous American species of Clematis, sometimes referred to as Atragene, that are well worth

growing. Our Traveler's Joy, *C. virginiana,* found glori-
fying the roadside tangle in the late summer with its
crowding, creamy blooms, is not of the first merit for
garden use, though it may be transplanted from the
wild to disguise unsightly objects or for trailing over a
wall or a stump. It lacks the delicious vanilla scent that
augments the charms of the Japanese *Clematis paniculata,* which it otherwise resembles. Other Clematises
of the *paniculata* type are the fragrant Virgin's Bower
of the Mediterranean region, *C. Flammula,* and the
vigorous *C. Vitalba,* of British hedgerows. All these are
desirable, bearing a profusion of creamy flowers in
panicles and climbing high.

   C. coccinea (*C. texensis*), a species native in Texas,
is a slender climber of great interest and distinction.
Its leaves are slightly glaucous and for a long period
in spring it hangs out scarlet urn-shaped flowers in
generous numbers. I grew this species from seed and
allowed it to share a cedar post with a white Rose with
which it got on admirably. It climbs little more than six
feet high. *C. crispa* is another extremely pretty American species found in Virginia and the Southwest. The
flowers are sweet-scented and in various tones of blue-
purple, and are borne over most of the summer. Allowed
to clamber over a bush, or swinging from the cross-
piece of a cedar pergola, this is an attractive and graceful species, and easily grown. It may be purchased or
raised from seed.

   Dr. Spingarn published in the January, 1934, number
of the *National Horticultural Magazine* an article en-
titled, "American Clematis for American Gardens: A
Brief Account of All Species Native to the United States

and Their Use in Gardens." The reader will be astonished to find how rich this country is in Clematis species. Many of them sound highly desirable, and the lover of this beautiful race will undoubtedly set out forthwith to add some of them to his garden treasury.

There are so many desirable foreign-born species that it is not possible to do more than make a selection among them for discussion here. Taken alphabetically, the first is *C. alpina,* found in some seed lists under the name of *Atragene alpina.*

C. alpina is the earliest species to open its blossoms, save the winter-flowering kinds, which are not hardy in the North. It is found at high elevations in the mountains of Europe and is quite hardy where other conditions are to its mind. Mr. Robinson recommends for it a northern exposure and a peaty soil, though undoubtedly lime should be added to the soil. Though a climber, it does not aspire to any great height, growing slenderly from four to six feet tall. The fragile nodding blossoms are a delicate lilac-blue. This species is very useful in the rougher parts of the rock garden, where it may be allowed to trail over bushes or large stones.

C. calycina (*C. balearica*) and *C. cirrhosa* are evergreen climbers, not hardy in the locality of New York; indeed, they require a much milder climate, and the latter form is sometimes grown as a greenhouse plant. But for southern gardens they would be an admirable addition, blooming as they do in winter. The first is native in Minorca, and has bell-shaped greenish flowers spotted with color; the second is found in southern Europe and North Africa, and the creamy flowers are

sweet-scented. M. Correvon offers seed of *C. cirrhosa.*
C. montana, and especially its lovely variety *C. m.
rubens,* are splendid hardy climbers. The flowers, which
are profusely borne, are the size and shape of a Japanese
Anemone, and delightfully sweet-scented. The variety
rubens is the hardier and more lovely of the two, the
blossoms being of a soft orchid pink. These bloom at
Tulip time, and a wall hung with them makes a fine
background for masses of lavender, pink, and white
Tulips. A form known as *Wilsoni* is said to be particularly fine, but I have not seen it. *C. Spooneri* is one of
the late Dr. Wilson's introductions from China. It is
closely related to *C. montana* and is a vigorous kind
with white blossoms. All these are lovely for planting
against Apple trees, where they clamber among the
open branches and hang in festoons of amazing grace.
Of this group also is *C. Fargesi,* a hardy species blooming at midsummer.

Several yellow-flowered species are attractive and
well worth growing. I first saw yellow Clematises many
years ago in Miss Willmott's garden at Warley. I have
since grown from seed *C. orientalis* (*C. graveolens*),
an Asiatic species with small, pale yellow, sweetly
fragrant urn-shaped blossoms and a somewhat rampant,
though not excessive, habit of growth. *C. tangutica,*
found in a wild state in Mongolia and western China,
is a finer plant altogether, however. This, too, I have
raised from seed. The blossoms are larger and of a
purer yellow than those of any other yellow-flowered
species I have met with, more or less urn-shaped and
long and pointed, and are carried free of the foliage on
six-inch stalks. It is absolutely hardy.

C. nutans is another yellow-flowered species native in the Himalayas, the blossoms of which are said to have a delightful Cowslip fragrance. It would be valuable, for it flowers in autumn; but I have not yet found seed of it.

C. Viticella is a native of southern Europe and has grown in gardens for several hundred years. It has rich purple flowers of flat shape and good size. I have found the varieties derived from this species the easiest of the large-flowered kinds to deal with. The variety *kermesina* is a delightful wine-red in color and blooms from June throughout August.

We have not at our command the vast number of large-flowered Clematises offered in foreign catalogues, but a very good selection may be made. Ramona, *Henryi, Jackmani,* Mme. Baron Veillard, Mme. Edouard André, Ville de Lyon, and the double-flowered and sweetly scented Duchess of Edinburgh are all lovely and to be had. Grow them with climbing Roses, and no effect could be lovelier.

CHAPTER XXV

As surely as seasons wax and wane the gardener is confronted with the time when he must "do something" to that most troublesome adjunct of the garden, the herbaceous border. Each of us who has looked his borders fairly in the face this summer (and not as a mother regards a beloved child, with excuses on her lips and infinite tolerance in her heart) is less than satisfied. For when is a herbaceous border wholly satisfactory? Almost never!

I am not sure but that I should call the herbaceous border the bad child of the garden, so seldom does it come up to our expectations, so almost invariably does it disappoint us and flout our utmost efforts to perfect it. The trouble is, as it is so often with the unruly child, we expect something of it that it simply cannot be. We expect it to present to us for at least five months of the year—May, June, July, August, and September—a radiant and flawless face. This, in our climate where prolonged droughts and torrid heat rush the plants in and out of bloom with disconcerting speed, and torrential rains thrash the flowers to a pulp and lay low the strongest stalks, is a well-nigh impossible accomplishment. Even in the British Isles, where the herbaceous border is at its best because the garden practitioners have reached a high degree of skill in this branch of their art, and where the climate is more gentle-tempered, it is not the easily turned trick it seems to envious beholders from our shores. Even there subterfuges must be resorted to. With my own eyes I have seen (even in Miss Jekyll's matchless garden) pots of Lilies and annuals in full bloom being craftily dropped into such sections of the border as have failed to come up to standard.

I don't know any reasons why this practice is not playing the garden game in a perfectly legitimate way, but somehow one always has a sense of its being not quite fair. In any case it is an expensive ruse, or expedient, necessitating glass and gardeners and what not—things which most of us are rather short on.

The herbaceous border, it seems to me, should be made to stand on its own merits, and we, perhaps, should be satisfied with something less than perfection. There will be periods in every carefully made border when it will smile graciously from end to end, but (unless we practice expert pot-dropping) there will also be periods when it will be not so good.

At any rate there is always something that may be done to improve it. Once in every three or four years the border should be completely turned out, redug and refertilized, the plants rearranged. This is preferably done in early spring. In the autumn the most we can do is to pick out the most glaring defects and remedy them to the best of our knowledge and ability. There will be, at whatever season the work of improvement is undertaken, a certain amount of elimination to be done; some plants will have proved unworthy in our sight, or have turned out to be depredatory weeds. Such should be torn out and thrown upon the rubbish heap. Do not worry along with plants you do not admire, or that give you unnecessary trouble. Of some fast spreaders you may be very fond, and these, such as the Helianthuses, Boltonias, and Bocconias, will need drastic curbing. Seedlings of Phlox, Coreopsis, Hollyhocks, Foxgloves, and the like will have sprung up in the wrong places. These, save the Phlox seedlings which will invariably turn out to be worthless, may be transplanted to situations where they will be effective. Certain clumps of Phlox, Moonpenny Daisies, Delphiniums, Pyrethrums, and Campanulas, will require to be divided and reset. Do not hesitate to discard the old spent portions; retain only the young and vigorous growths from the outside of the clump. Loosely woven clumps, such as Heucheras, some Campanulas, Moonpenny Daisies, may be pulled apart with the fingers; for heavy, tight clumps of Phlox, Hemerocallis, Delphinium, a sharp knife will be required, or two hand forks may be inserted back to back in the clump and pressed together to wrench it apart. Biennials, if they have bloomed, will have disappeared, and their places must be filled.

Thus we shall have two things especially in mind in this autumn renovation: the filling of blank spaces left by death or removal, and the addition of plants to the portions of the border that need pepping up and toning down. In these operations we shall of course keep in mind the pleasing association of colors, whether in harmony or in contrast, and the agreeable juxtaposition of plants of contrasting foliage and habit. In illustration of this latter dictum such examples as the associations of Iris and Lupine may be cited, or of Japanese Iris and Astilbe, Hosta and Gypsophila, Baptisia and Thermopsis.

A little well rotted manure, bonemeal, or other fertilizer may be worked into the soil as the renovation goes forward.

Here are a few suggestions that may easily be carried out:

A pleasant variation in our Tulip groupings may be made if the bulbs of the May-flowering varieties are interplanted with Camassias, or with the Spanish Blue-bell, *Scilla campanulata.* Camassias come in tones of lavender, pale and deep, and in pure white. The star-flowered stalks top those of the Tulips. *Scilla campanulata* comes in tones of blue, rose and in pure white. It is not as tall as the Tulips, and one looks down among the gorgeous cups to see the forest of belled spikes.

It is not wise to plant bulbs directly along the edges of the herbaceous borders, for, however delightful the effect may be at the time of their blossoming, there is always their untidy going off that offends the eye of the fastidious gardener. They may be planted thickly among the clumps of perennials so that their last state may be covered by a kindly veil of oncoming green.

The edge of a border, like the hem of a skirt, should be neat, though not necessarily even. Some persons like to edge their borders with long-blooming annuals, such as Sweet Alyssum. But for those who like a permanent edge here are three solutions: Alternating plants of white *Dianthus plumarius, Campanula carpa-*

tica (both the blue and the white forms) and Heuchera in tones of pink and coral. Allow each plant about ten inches of space. This edging gives a very long period of bloom and harmonizes with anything that may occupy the space behind it. Edgings of *Nepeta Mussini* and *Cerastium tomentosum* are also attractive; or of the Nepeta and *Dianthus plumarius*, preferably some white form, allowing one plant of Nepeta to five of the Dianthus. These last two combinations are attractive and seemly even when out of bloom, for the soft gray foliage makes a nice setting for the bright flowers in the border.

Another part of the border that requires careful planting is where it may make a sharp turn. Here one of the Funkias (Hosta), preferably *F. subcordata*, with frosted white flowers, or *F. Sieboldiana*, with steel-blue leaves and blue flowers, is well placed with a grouping of Gypsophila Bristol Fairy, or *Geranium sanguineum album*, both of spreading habit and long-lasting gossamer beauty, behind. One of the large-leaved Saxifrages or Aster Mauve Cushion may be substituted for the Funkia. The one blooms very early in spring, the other in autumn, while the Funkia is intermediate, but all keep to the end of the season a tidy and seemly front.

Clumps of double-flowered Pyrethrums are beautiful in the early summer garden towards the front of the borders, and blocks of Sweet Williams always make a lovely show in the June garden. A good companion for either Newport Pink or Newport Scarlet Sweet William is the lavender-flowered Erigeron Quakeress. The plants of this should be supported by pieces of twiggy brush inserted inconspicuously among the growths.

The blood-red Sweet William known as *nigricans,* that has blackish purple stems and leaves, will do wonders in subduing the raw color of that good perennial, *Lychnis chalcedonica,* if planted beside it. There is a light salmon-colored form of this Lychnis that I have used with nice effect next to Japanese Iris in lavender and purple tones. Certain of the herbaceous Spiraeas and Astilbes make good foils for Japanese Iris and enjoy the same dampish soil conditions.

A group of *Scabiosa japonica* with soft lavender flowers in front of the yellow-flowered *Aquilegia chrysantha* makes a fine near-front picture with a long season of bloom—June to August. If you have a planting of *Anchusa italica* that does not please you, interplant it with the old Garden Heliotrope, *Valeriana officinalis,* and set in front of it a mass of *Anthemis tinctoria,* either the bright yellow *Kelwayi* or the pale E. C. Buxton. The Anthemis should be supported, as we suggested for Erigeron, so that the many branches may assume a natural pose. They should never be gathered together and fastened to a single stake.

Delphiniums have two time-honored companions— *Lilium candidum* and *Lilium croceum.* But they should also have the charming foil of *Thalictrum glaucum,* as I have noted elsewhere, with its lovely gray leaves and puffs of pale yellow bloom. Thermopsis is good with Delphinium, especially for cutting, and *Campanula latifolia macrantha,* rich purple or pure white, though blossoming first, remains to make an interesting association with them.

Autumn Aid for Perennial Borders

The beauty of Eryngiums and the white *Malva moschata alba* has often been noted. Stokesia has a long period of bloom towards the front of a sunny border, and either the blue or the white form is good with a background of Sidalcea, white or rose, which will begin to flower first.

Campanula lactiflora follows the Delphiniums and makes a fine background planting for groups of late-flowering Hemerocallis and *Veronica spicata*. Another effective midsummer group is composed of the white Mullein, Verbascum Miss Willmott, the purple Loosestrife, and in the foreground the white form of *Agrostemma coronaria*, with its soft gray velvet leaves.

The Phlox masses usually require to be broken up with plants of other forms, such as Globe Thistles (Echinops), Eryngiums, Artemisia Silver King and *A. lactiflora*, Lyme Grass (Elymus), *Veronica virginica* and *V. subsessilis*, Sea Lavender, the Funkias (Hostas), and the white Gooseneck-flower, *Lysimachia clethroides*.

Hollyhocks are well companioned at the back of the border with *Bocconia cordata*, or the tall white Mullein, and in front of them may be a mass planting of Phlox Miss Lingard interplanted with the lovely pink and coral-colored forms of *Pentstemon barbatus* for earlier bloom, or of *Lavatera Olbia* with *Galega Hartlandii;* this last a pleasant association in pink and lavender and white.

Lilium Henryi towers handsomely behind a planting of *Salvia virgata nemorosa,* and a group of *Lilium tigrinum* is greatly improved by being interplanted with *Aconitum Napellus bicolor.* In making use of *Aconitum Wilsonii* it should be remembered that, though it is so tall as to belong at the back of the border, it is too slender to make a proper background plant and itself needs a backing of wall or tall hedge or some good shrub.

Where the two biennials, Foxgloves and Canterbury Bells, bloomed earlier, there will now be blank spaces. It is a good plan to set behind these plants Asters of the *ericoides* group, or other wandlike species, so that they may be drawn down to cover the defection.

We need not, I think, fash ourselves overmuch about colors, for living colors do not clash in the same way as do stuffs, or what might be called dead hues. Certain juxtapositions of course are bad, and these are easily taken care of; but on the whole, with plenty of green and a sense of proportion in the use of color, there will be little trouble.

CHAPTER XXVI

COLCHICUMS FOR AUTUMN PLEASURE

MEETING new persons, entertaining new ideas, viewing new scenes, lend zest and freshness to life. The gardener finds this same zest in making the acquaintance of plants that are new to him. To look forward to the blossoming of a dozen or so different plants or shrubs that he has not met before, especially if their habits, appearances, and forbearances are unknown to him, is as effective as an excursion abroad in quickening his imagination and refreshing his spirit. Old friends are indispensable, but new ones keep us alert—so in the garden.

Colchicums, though long grown in gardens, are still not common, at least in this country. And this is rather surprising since they are easy to grow and may be made to play a quite important part in the bravura of the autumn garden. Autumn Crocuses, a few kinds, are quite well known, but Colchicums, which resemble them, are seldom seen in any save the gardens of the curious, or in botanical collections. Some years ago on a misty September morning I saw these flowers for the first time in the rock garden of the Edinburgh Botanic Garden. I thought them Crocuses, though some were pinker than any Crocus with which I was familiar. The labels soon put me right. These were Colchicums,

[221]

these flowers thrusting up innocent of leaves at the base of giant rocks in little shimmering colonies. I was enchanted with them and have since pursued Colchicums with assiduity, though rather hobbled by the plant quarantine, that lets in Crocuses but inexplicably excludes Colchicums.

A little research revealed them as a genus belonging to the Lily family, differing from Crocus (which is a member of the Iris clan) "in three main characters, the position of the ovary, the number of the stamens (a Crocus has only three stamens while a Colchicum has six) and also of the styles." The non-botanical observer may note more superficial differences—chiefly a certain lack of that pristine crispness that is the property of all Crocuses, and a sort of carelessness of port, so to speak, which is more in the character of Bulbocodium, a still less well known bulbous plant. Colchicum is allied to Bulbocodium but differs from this little spring flower in the possession of six stamens and three styles, and the segments are not, as in Bulbocodium, "divided right down to the top of the ovary instead of being joined to form a perianth tube."

In ancient works, Colchicums are called Meadow Saffrons, or occasionally "Sonne before the Father, because (as they thinke) it giveth seede before the flower." But this notion, as the old writer goes on to explain, is credited only by those who do not give the matter due consideration. When the bulb is planted the blossoms spring up, then in spring the leaves appear and the seed, concealed in the ovary below ground, ripens before the leaves fade in June. The corm matures soon

after. From its unusual habit of flowering without leaves the Colchicum has also been called Naked Boys or Naked Ladies.

The leaves, as I have said, make their appearance in spring, very early, and grow with prodigious speed to a height in some species of two feet, bushy and lush and superbly, if inconveniently, exuberant. And herein lies their one drawback. For one looking upon the lovely rosy or white goblets in autumn gets no hint of this passionately leafy aftermath and so is careless of setting the corms in positions where there is room for them. And then when the great sheaves of leaves push up in spring one is astonished and put out, and when in June they begin to turn yellow and lie about, staging disorderly and unseemly deathbed scenes, one is quite properly outraged and resolves to have no more to do with such coarse creatures, which are probably not only quite out of scale with their surroundings but have, moreover, undoubtedly flopped over your choicest treasures and caused them to die. But before you root them out and cast them on the rubbish heap I pray you let your mind drift back to the autumn days when their naked blowing above the drowsing earth seemed a very miracle, and I am sure you will find some other way out of the dilemma.

Colchicums are definitely not for use in small rock gardens. In my own they are grown at the back in a sort of no-man's land where the soil is black and rich, among Pulmonarias, Mertensias, Celandines, *Anchusa myosotidiflora* and mats of Arabis, a region wherein they can do no harm, for their companions are well able to take care of themselves, and this situation is not generally visible and need not be looked at unless it is in good blossoming. Also we grow them along the edge of a shrubbery border in clumps—and this is generally the best place for them.

Colchicums should be planted in August, so send in your order in plenty of time. They like a deep rich soil, a nice loam not too dry, and it must be remembered that they suffer in times of drought and should be given water freely. They like sunshine, but a little shade for part of the day is not detrimental to them. The individual flowers do not last long, but they follow one another in quick succession, a well grown corm sending up many flowers. The bulbs should be set about three inches deep over all. Violets of sorts make a good ground cover for them, protecting the delicate blossoms from spattering mud in the autumn storms. They may also be planted in grass but the increase in such situations will be slow. The hues of Colchicums vibrate from purest white through faint blush to deep rose-lavender, almost garnet, the blooms of some species being tessellated or checkered in two tones. These checkered forms were much admired of old, and John Rea, in his "Flora" says that "such as bear single flowers wholly of one color, and neither striped, or checkered, we will pass over as not worth the trouble." But today we do not agree with the old seventeenth century gardener, and think the pure whites and the selfs the prettiest of all. If the different species are planted, they make gentle gaiety in the garden from the end of August through October.

And now for the kinds. As I have said, we are hindered by the plant quarantine from easily forming a collection; but quite a number are to be had in this country nevertheless.

Colchicum autumnale is perhaps the easiest to grow, though few are difficult, and it is the easiest to procure. Its flowers are about two inches in length and of starry form, a pale uniform lilac in the type, but there is a lovely pure white form that is generously floriferous of fluffy white blossoms that are, however, somewhat smaller than those of the type. There are several other forms of *autumnale* well worth growing. One with faint stripes on the pale ground would have pleased the critical eye of old John Rea, and another that was greatly admired by Parkinson, who described it as a pale purple on its first coming forth but after a few days "becoming to bee a very deepe reddish-purple color, as also the little foot-stalk on which it doth stand."

Very beautiful when well grown is the double white form, *C. autumnale album plenum*. In good forms the flowers are snowy white with a faint flesh tint at the heart, the many petals long and narrow. The double form of the type is also good to look upon. This is *C. a. flora pleno*. These double forms last a long time in perfection, and the white one always commands a distressingly high price. *C. autumnale* flowers late in September and in early October, sending up flower after flower with ardent generosity. A form called *major* is larger-flowered, "massive blooms of rosy purple," and is popular for indoor growing. There is also *C. a. minor* (*C. Balansae*) which may be had in this country, a flower of somewhat greater substance than the pale rosy-lilac type and with more rounded segments.

What Happens in My Garden

Colchicum autumnale is common in rich meadow-
land in many parts of England, especially in limestone
districts. It is said to be poisonous to cattle, but Mr.
Bowles reports that after some research he has been
unable to hear of instances of actual cattle poisoning.
Ann Pratt, however, gives numerous instances of death
both to cattle and to humans from eating Colchicum.
The corm is the basis of a medicine long used in the
relief of gout. This is the sole British species.

C. alpinum is the smallest of the species and the first
to bloom, often making its appearance in early August.
It is not often seen in cultivation, and I know of no
firm offering it in this country. Mr. Bowles calls it the
most delicately beautiful of autumnal bulbous plants.
A pity that we may not have it. Visitors to the Alps,
to Mt. Cenis, or to various high regions of Italy,
Switzerland, or Sicily may come upon its charming inch-
high pinky-lilac bubbles thrusting through the grasses.
The foliage of *C. alpinum* consists of but two narrow,
inconspicuous leaves. It is said not to be easy to satisfy.

Colchicum speciosum and its varieties offer to the
late September and October garden much opulent
beauty. It bears very large and handsome flowers,
which from a well developed bulb measure almost a
foot in length; Mr. Farrer describes the color as claret-
rose. They are somewhat bowl-shaped, swelling in
delicate symmetry from their slender tubes to a graciously rounded form almost three inches across. The
flowers have a faint, rather medicinal odor. This
species is found in the Caucasus, Macedonia, and as
far east as Persia. There are numerous forms of it.
C. s. album is strikingly beautiful. I cannot do better

than quote Mr. Bowles as to its charms: "The snow-white goblets of good form, equal to that of a Tulip, standing on soft emerald-green tubes cannot be equalled for beauty in the late autumn by any other plant so easy to grow well in the autumn. Its only rivals among white flowers are *Romneya Coulteri* and *Crinum Powellii album,* which, however, have generally left the field clear for the Colchicum before its flowering season commences." Unfortunately the corms of this treasure remain expensive.

Belonging to this same general group is *C. Bornmulleri,* larger of flower and even more glorious than *C. speciosum.* It flowers before *autumnale* in September, continuing throughout the month in a manner to delight the soul. The flowers are a most delicate rose-lilac as they open, white at the base and rising on clear green tubes that never become suffused with the body color of the flower, though this slowly deepens with maturity. Before the great blossoms have faded the observant gardener will note the tips of next year's leaves and the spathes peeping from the soil about the base of the flowers.

C. giganteum, called a "grand species from Zigana Dagh (Gypsy Mountain) in Asia Minor," also bears immense lilac flowers. It has a white or pale yellow throat. This species and *C. Bornmulleri* are deliciously and quite surprisingly fragrant. They have the smell of honey, or of Sweet Alyssum after rain.

Of the tessellated or checkered group *C. agrippinum* is the only one I have so far grown. Its checkers are less distinct that those of *C. Sibthorpii,* which to my knowledge is not offered in this country. *C. variegatum* is also more distinctly checkered. Both these last-named kinds are found in Greece and the islands of the Archipelago. The native habitat of *C. agrippinum* is not known, and it is probably a natural hybrid. It blooms early in the autumn, hoisting its vaguely checkered flowers on long slender tubes. The leaves are long and stand nearly erect. It is an easily grown kind, but where the climate is severe it is grateful for a blanket of leaves or salt hay.

Mr. van Tubergen of Haarlem, Holland, has lately interested himself in the introduction of some excellent hybrid Colchicums, some of which we are fortunate enough to be able to procure in this country. The names of these hybrids are given below with the dealer's descriptions, but as these descriptions do not exactly tally with the flowers as they are labeled in my garden I cannot wholly vouch for them. The confusion in labeling may have occurred here or at the dealer's. All the kinds, however, are very effective and well worth growing under any name. They are:

Autumn Queen, deep rose-purple
Mr. Kerbert, pale rose-violet
Violet Queen, lilac-tinted violet
Lilac Wonder, pinky-lavender
Premier, dark lilac
The Giant, very large lilac flower
Conquest, dark violet
President Coolidge, light violet.

Bulbs should be ordered early in the summer, and request made for early delivery. If the bulbs are planted as soon as received a most unexpected pleasure will be enjoyed for many weeks during the autumn.

The flowers endure weather conditions with amazing fortitude; especially are the double-flowered sorts hardy and resistant. Last autumn the double-flowered form of *C. autumnale* continued to send up perfect flowers after many hard frosts. I think it must have been in bloom for more than six weeks.

Of course, this is to say very little about this fascinating genus. I have not touched at all upon the group that flower with the leaves in winter or very early spring. But these difficult and chancy things are almost impossible for us to procure. They are found in eastern Europe, Syria, Asia Minor, North Africa, and a rare yellow-flowered kind in Afghanistan. We need not weep for them at present but can satisfy ourselves with the wealth that is at hand. I want to say again, if you do not know Colchicums, give yourself this pleasure at once.

CHAPTER XXVII

DOVECOTES AND GARDENS

In "The Fragrant Path" attention is called to the comely appropriateness of certain old-fashioned garden accessories, chiefly the long line of white-painted bee-hives, or the brightly colored straw bee skeps, that endowed gardens of an unpretentious character with a charm not always imparted by more elaborate furnishings. Among these old-fashioned adjuncts was also the dovecote, and this was not by any means confined to gardens of modest pretensions; for when designed by an artist and placed with discrimination it may be made to fit into a garden of almost any type.

Any one who is familiar with the older English and French gardens has noted how often a dovecote is to be found as part of the garden scheme, or placed just without the walls in the field or fold. Usually these ancient erections are beautiful in line and exceedingly picturesque in effect. In early times, before cattle and sheep raising was general or on a large scale in England, pigeons formed a most important article of diet; and so pigeon houses, or columbaries, as they were called, were quite indispensable to every country place, and immense flocks of the prolific birds were kept in order to supply the household's demand for fresh meat. Ancient cookbooks abound in recipes for cook-

ing pigeons. One such old work that I have at hand
gives twenty-seven distinct ways of preparing pigeons
for the table, including the still popular and toothsome
pigeon pie and the once famous and very elaborate dish
known as jugged pigeon.

In very early times, however, even as late as the
spacious days of Queen Elizabeth—indeed, in some
localities until the reign of James I—the right to erect
a columbary and to keep pigeons was accorded only
to privileged classes, the great lords of manors, wealthy
landowners, and to high dignitaries of the Church. This
was true in France as well as in England. And it was
estimated by that eminent agriculturist and friend of
Milton, Samuel Hartlib, that toward the middle of the
seventeenth century there were no fewer than twenty-
six thousand dovecotes in England. Huge flocks of
birds were kept, anywhere from five hundred to a
thousand pairs to a cote; and these vast numbers of
birds belonging to the great fed voraciously upon the
crops of the poor and humble, for which hardship the
latter had no redress whatever.

The oldest form of dovecote found in England is
Norman in origin, a massive circular building with
walls three feet or more in thickness and a low-domed,
vaulted roof, windowless, and with no means of en-
trance for the birds save a round hole in the center of
the roof, which also admitted a modicum of light and
air. There is a famous example of such a circular dovecote at Athelhampton Hall in Dorset, England, which
many visitors to that lovely garden will call to mind.
It stands in the paddock by the stream—or so I remember it. The interior of this house is arranged in tiers of

L-shaped nests built into the solid stone walls from floor to roof. In the center is a curious contraption called in France a "portence" which enables the egg or squab gatherer to reach all the nests without difficulty. A ladder is hung from a cross arm that is set in a socket in the center of the house, and by turning the post the ladder is quite easily moved along the nest-filled walls.

As time went on the circular dovecote was replaced by various other forms which materialized in all sorts of shapes and designs, hardly two alike, though among the most popular styles were the simple square house and that of octagonal shape, often with a gabled roof surmounted by a lantern or again by a small cupola, which served as an open-air dovecote, with an ornamental weathervane atop. Stone was the most commonly employed material, but in certain sections the lovely "black and white" construction of oaken beams and "wattle and daub," that we know as half-timbered work, was used with fine effect.

As persons of lesser degree were permitted to keep pigeons many houses of simpler design made their appearance. One of the most popular of these was the barrel dovecote, sometimes called a pole-house. This was a circular house, usually made of wood, raised upon a stout pole. Such a house was frequently set up in old gardens as the centerpiece of a pattern of flower-filled beds and grass paths, and so it could be most effectively used today.

The gabled house also makes a pretty and appropriate garden feature, and one that may easily be constructed by any one with a knack of carpentry.

Dovecotes and Gardens

Sometimes the end of a brick garden wall is finished off with a simply designed dovecote in the same material and with a shingled roof. Formerly also the gabled end of an English farmhouse was pierced with holes to admit pigeons that made their homes in the loft behind. We see the effect copied today sometimes, but the openings are merely used with decorative intent. Modern ideas of sanitation would preclude a loft full of pigeons, often infested with vermin, above the dwelling rooms, but in the careless days of our forefathers this appeared a thrifty way of utilizing otherwise wasted spaces.

Herb gardens are happily again coming into fashion and into use, and it seems to me that no prettier or more appropriate accessory could be found to enhance the Old World atmosphere of these fragrant enclosures than a dovecote. It might be a small barrel type that would lend itself as a central feature of a neat pattern of little beds and narrow paths, or a gabled house placed at the end of a straight path. And the pigeons with their gentle voices and soft fluttering ways would be an added attraction. Here too they would find something to their taste, for Cummin seed, always to be found in a properly furnished herb garden, "hath always," according to an old book, "been esteemed a famous drawer of pigeons"; and in that cheerful long ago of which we are writing, it was, you must know, a perfectly justifiable and even laudable feature of the pigeon fancying game to draw your neighbor's birds from his cote to your own by whatever means you could devise. One simple method was to anoint the birds with myrrh which caused others to leave home and follow them, but it was thought even more certain to mix with their food a little sweet wine and Cummin seed, which so perfumed their breath as to make them irresistible to all birds that came near them.

I once saw in England a round stone dovecote used with delightful effect as the focal point in the center of a formal Rose garden. Height was thereby given to this too often flat and featureless area, and the snowy King pigeons that fluttered murmurously above the roof or arose in graceful flight against the sky brought life and vivacity to the galaxy of impassive beauties in the geometrical beds.

When the colonists came to America it may be imagined that they reveled in the chance to keep pigeons, as well as in the great flocks of wild ones that haunted the countryside. These were killed in thousands every year and put down in lard to provide fresh meat for winter consumption. Today the extermination of the wild pigeons is believed to be complete. Here and there in America old dovecotes are to be found, though. The fine brick one at Shirley-on-James in Virginia is a notable example, but it is probable that the majority of them were not built of such durable material and so have perished.

In a short chapter one cannot say much as to pigeon-keeping in general, but something should be said of the beauty of the individual kinds; for even in the old days pigeons were not kept for their "advantage" alone, but many for the sake of "their largeness of Body and their beauty and diversity of Colours." And a dovecote without the gentle voices and ceaseless movement of its rightful tenants would surely have little meaning or reason for being.

The fancy of some will run to extraordinary types of pigeons—to the proud inflated Pouters, or those strangely possessed Tumblers that have the incomprehensible habit of tumbling backwards during flight; to the beautiful strutting Fantails, the Frillbacks, the Crowned Pigeons, or the Jacobins, with the feathers of the neck forming a demure hood and with long wings and tail.

CHAPTER XXVIII

A WHITE GARDEN IN WALES

At the center of each man's being, says Chesterton, is a dream. My pet dream for many years has been a white garden, set apart and inclosed within a shining green hedge. I never have come anywhere near to realizing this dream, never had space enough to be anything so special—or perhaps it is horticultural self-control that has been lacking. Something. But since the mild summer evening on which I once saw a white garden beautifully carried out it has lingered in my mind as indeed "such stuff as dreams are made on," and one of the loveliest gardens I ever saw.

This white garden was one of a series of gardens on a splendid estate in Wales, on the river Ely, not far from ancient Llandaff. It was planted entirely with white-flowering plants and inclosed, not in the close-clipped hedges of my desire, but by stone walls of a warm pinkish gray. This was not, as might be supposed, cold in effect; the curious hue of the stone was warm and almost luminous and made a delightful background for the pale flowers. We saw this garden first at twilight, that witching hour, and through the tall iron gates, above which swung a Clematis starred with immense white blooms, the effect was almost as if a mist had crept up from the river and finding the haven of this quiet inclosure had swirled around and about, rising here in wraith spires and turrets, lying there in gauzy breadths amidst the muted green. It is impossible to describe its beauty at this dim hour— so soft, so ethereal, so mysterious, half real it seemed. And yet when we saw it at noon of the next day it was no less arresting, though in a different way. It had become, so to speak, flesh and blood. Something you could draw boldly near to. Looking at it, we did not speak in whispers as we had done the night before.

Now it would be natural to suppose that a garden planted wholly with white flowers would be bleak in effect, or at least very monotonous; but this was not at all the case. It was neither funereal nor weddingish in appearance. It was frank and fresh and full of changing values. At twilight, of course, it seemed a little unreal, but isn't that true of almost any garden at this hour when the hand of man is less apparent and mysterious agencies seem to have brought it into being? There are, as a matter of fact, almost no *pure* white flowers. I have seen Sweet Peas of an absolutely flat paper-whiteness, but for the moment I can call to mind no other flowers of such unrelieved pallor. A large proportion of so-called white flowers tend towards buff, or mauve or blush in the throat; the petals of many are delicately lined, or veined or blotched with color —blue, carmine, green, yellow. A great number are not white at all but what we call cream-white, blush-white or skimmed-milk white, and the name of those having a greenish cast is legion. Many flowers change from white to pink or even to deep rose or yellow as they age, while bunches of bright-hued stamens or stigmata often cast a glow over the whole flower. Things being as they are, there could not possibly be monotony of tone in a garden of white flowers.

And there is besides infinite diversity of texture; there will be the flat sheenless whites, the satin whites, the velvet whites, while the variety of form is as great as among other flowers—spires, wedges, flat corymbs, spikes, bursts of mist, trails, streamers, banners, and plumes, they lie along the ground, aspire slenderly, climb the walls and trellises, are hung from tree and shrub in infinite multiformity and contrast. And in addition the foliage of the different plants and shrubs offers its own contrastive spice—the dark and light and yellow-greens with the many gray and silvery tones of the leaves quite preventing any monotonous duplication or harping recurrence of hue. It was plain, however, that this Welsh garden was the product of the most loving care and intelligent choice of material.

At the back of the garden, which was in the form of a large rectangle, a raised rectangular stone pool with a broad coping interrupted the wide border against the wall. The pool was lined with the palest sea-blue tiles, and out of a spray of carved (stone, I think) Lilies in the center a slender jet of water arose high in the air and swayed this way and that like a dancer in the wind, falling back finally with a light whisper into the clear waters of the basin. At the corners on the wide coping stood large tubs filled with white Lilies of the Nile.

The border that extended around the inclosure only interrupted by the pool and the gateway was about seven feet wide. The flowers were all congregated here, leaving the heavy velvet turf of the rest of the inclosure unbroken save that just off the center a very old Thorn tree spread its dark crooked branches, and in its shadow a little iron table and a few comfortable seats were casually placed. The suggestion of tea and pleasant loitering in this peaceful, fragrant spot was very agreeable.

It was midsummer when we saw this white garden in Wales, and the flowers that held the stage at this season were chiefly great masses of wedge-headed Phloxes, tall and dwarf, the tall spires of Chimney and other Bellflowers, Boltonias, white Lilies, annuals in a wide variety, including Sweet Peas that were supported on trellises at the back of the border, Gladioli and Dahlias, and a few shrubs. The borders were edged with stone, and spilling over this confining band in masses were white annual Pinks, Phlox Drummondii, Cupflower, Petunias, frilly and plain, Verbenas, pale California Poppies, Sweet Alyssum, Carpathian Harebells, Heuchera, Flaxflowers, and the like. Here and there a climber came from the outer side and flung itself over the rim of the wall in tangled masses or long streamers, and more than one lingering Rose pressed a satin cheek against the warm-hued stone.

A chief and very apparent charm of this white garden was its sweetness, for many white flowers are fragrant, especially towards night. At dusk the perfumes arising from white Tobacco, Stock, Lilies, the masses of gray-white Heliotrope, Tuberoses, and Petunias were almost overpowering. And besides the fragrant flowers I noticed that a thoughtful hand had set among them plants of Lemon Verbena, Sweet Geranium, Southernwood, Rosemary, Lavender, *Cedronella triphylla,* and other plants beloved for their scented leaves.

We talked with the gardener in charge and learned that this garden was cunningly planted to be as full of bloom as possible throughout the season and not, as is often the case with one-color gardens, for a short period only. Many spring- and summer-flowering bulbs were made use of, a wide range of annual and perennial plants, shrubs, climbers, and trees of medium height and gracious blossoming. Various devices were employed to maintain the continuous bloom. Annuals raised elsewhere were transplanted to blank spaces left by departed bulbs and to fill other gaps in the flowery procession; Lilies and Heliotropes and Tuberoses in pots were dropped in wherever they would do the most good. All withered or spent plants were immediately cleared away and replaced by something fresh. The British are clever at keeping a border always appearing at the peak of perfection, and their climate is their ally rather than their antagonist in this worthy aim.

I sat on one of the white seats in the midst of this gracious garden and rested my notebook on the little table while the friendly gardener patiently enumerated the plants he made use of to keep the borders always fresh and blossomy. This list I have changed a little, adding a few special favorites of my own and omitting certain plants that are unsuitable to our more severe climatic conditions, or that are at the present time unprocurable in this country. I give it here for the benefit of any who may be cherishing a similar dream to mine, or who may here and now give birth to one. I am sure a little inclosed white garden, or even a winding border of white flowers against a green background, would be a possession of which one would not easily tire. It would always suggest peace and harmony, yet there would be no lack of interest. Frayed nerves would find it remedial.

Shrubs or Small Trees to Be Used as Accents or Background

Spring-flowering: Amelanchier *canadensis,* 10 ft.; *Aronia arbutifolia,* 10 ft.; Chamaedaphne *calyculata,* 3 ft. evergreen; *Cornus florida,* 10–20 ft.; *C. Kousa,* 10–15 ft.; *Crataegus Oxyacantha* and *C. O. plena* (Hawthorn), 10–20 ft.; *Cytisus albus,* White Spanish Broom, 4–8 ft.; *C. kewensis,* low-growing; *Daphne Mezereum alba,* 4 ft. March; *Deutzia gracilis,* 1½ ft.; *D. Lemoinei; Exochorda grandiflora,* 10 ft.; *Halesia tetraptera,* 20 ft.; *Leucothoë Catesbaei* (evergreen), 4 ft.; *Lonicera bella albida,* 10 ft.; *L. fragrantissima,* 8 ft.; *L. Morrowi,* 12 ft.; *Magnolia conspicua,* 20 ft.; *M. stellata,* 8–10 ft.; *Philadelphus* (Mock Orange), many vars. tall and dwarf, single and double; *Pieris floribunda* and *P. japonica* (evergreen), 3–6 ft.; *Prunus glandulosa sinensis* (White-flowering Almond), 4–5 ft.; *P. maritima* (Beach Plum), 2–5 ft.; *P. tomentosa,* 5 ft.; *Prunus* (Cherry), Japanese vars., 20–30 ft.; *P. Persica flore-alboplena* (Peach); *Pyrus* (*Malus*) *baccata,* 20–30 ft.; *P. Sargenti,* 8 ft.; *P. toringoides,* 25 ft.; *Rhododendron carolinianum album,* 4–6 ft.; many hybrid vars.; *Rhodotypos kerrioides,* 5–6 ft.;

What Happens in My Garden

Rubus deliciosus, 3–6 ft.; *Spiraea arguta,* 6 ft.; *S. prunifolia,* 6 ft.; *S. Thunbergii,* 3–5 ft.; *S. Vanhouttei,* 8 ft.; *Viburnum Carlesii,* 3–5 ft.; *V. Lantana,* 15 ft.; *V. Lentago,* 20 ft.

Summer- and *autumn-flowering: Abelia chinensis,* 4 ft.; *Calluna vulgaris alba,* 15 ins.; *Ceanothus americanus,* 2–4 ft.; *Chionanthus virginica,* 15 ft.; *Cladrastis lutea,* 50 ft.; *Clethra alnifolia,* 4–8 ft.; *Cornus Nuttallii,* 8–10 ft.; *Deutzia scabra (crenata),* 8 ft.; *Hibiscus syriacus* Jeanne d'Arc (double), *H.* Snowstorm *(totus albus)* (single), 12 ft.; *Hydrangea arborescens grandiflora,* 5 ft.; *H. radiata,* 6 ft.; *Itea virginica,* 4 ft.; *Kalmia latifolia* (evergreen), 4–8 ft.; *Lonicera Ruprechtiana,* 12 ft.; *L. tatarica alba,* 10 ft.; *Rhododendron (Azalea) viscosum,* 4–6 ft.; *Rosa multiflora japonica,* 10 ft.; *R. rugosa alba* and vars., 5 ft.; *R. spinosissima,* 4–5 ft.; *Sambucus canadensis* (Elder), 10 ft.; *Syringa* (Lilac) *persica alba,* 8 ft.; *Syringa vulgaris* Frau Bertha Dammann, Marie Legraye, Jan van Tol (single), Edith Cavell, Mme. Casimir-Perier, Mme. Lemoine (double); *Viburnum americanum,* 12 ft.; *V. cassinoides,* 12 ft.; *V. tomentosum,* 8 ft.; *Weigela candida,* 7 ft.

Tall Plants for Use at Back of Border

Summer-flowering: Althaea rosea (Hollyhock), white vars., double and single; *Aruncus sylvester; Aster* Lady Trevellyn; *Bocconia cordata; Campanula lactiflora alba, C. pyramidalis alba; Cimicifuga simplex, C. racemosa; Delphinium,* white vars.; *Digitalis purpurea alba; Filipendula camtschatica (Spiraea gigantea); Iris ochroleuca (gigantea); Thalictrum aquilegifolium, T.*

cornuti, T. dipterocarpum album; Verbascum Miss Willmott.

Fall-flowering: Aster White Climax; *Boltonia asteroides; Chrysanthemum uliginosum; Phlox* Jeanne d'Arc; *Veronica virginica alba.*

Plants of Medium Height

Spring-flowering: Aquilegia nivea; Astilbe japonica; Dianthus barbatus album (Sweet William); *Hesperis matronalis alba; Iris florentina* and intermediate vars.; *Linum perenne album; Polemonium caeruleum album.*

Summer-flowering: Achillea Ptarmica Boule de Neige, *A. P.* Perry White; *Astilbe* Gerba d'Argent, *A.* Moerheim, *A. W. E.* Gladstone; *Campanula alliariaefolia, C. latifolia alba, C. Medium* (Canterbury Bells), *C. persicifolia alba; Centaurea montana alba; Centranthus ruber albus; Chelone glabra; Chrysanthemum maximum* vars.; *Clematis recta; Dictamnus; Filipendula hexapetala* (Dropwort), *F. Ulmaria* (Queen of the Meadow), *F. purpurea alba* (*Spiraea palmata*); *Galega officinalis alba; Geranium pratense album, G. sanguineum album; Gypsophila paniculata*, double and single; *Iris* (bearded), many vars.; *Iris* (Japanese); *Iris sibirica alba* and vars.; *Lobelia siphilitica alba; Lupinus polyphyllus albus; Monarda fistulosa alba; Oenothera speciosa; Papaver orientale* Perry's White; *Paeonia*, double and single, many vars.; *Pentstemon digitalis alba; Phlox* Frau Anton Buchner, *P.* Fräulein von Lassburg, *P.* Mrs. Jenkins, *P.* Miss Lingard; *Physostegia virginica alba; Platycodon grandiflorum album; Sidalcea candida; Stenanthium robustum; Tradescantia virginiana alba; Veronica longifolia alba, V. spicata alba; Yucca filamentosa.*

Fall-flowering: Anemone japonica Richard Ahrens, *A. j.* Whirlwind; *Aster* Snowflake; *Chrysanthemum coreanum, C.* Hardy Japanese; *Eupatorium Frazeri, E. ageratoides; Hosta plantaginea grandiflora* (Plantain Lily).

Low-Growing

Spring-flowering: Aquilegia flabellata nana-alba; Arenaria montana; Arabis albida and *A. a. fl.pl.; Asperula odorata; Cerastium tomentosum; Convallaria majalis* (Lily of the Valley); *Dianthus deltoides albus; Epimedium macranthum album; Erinus albus; Gypsophila cerastioides; Iberis sempervirens; Iris,* dwarf vars.; *Myosotis; Phlox divaricata alba, P. subulata Nelsonii; Primula polyantha* (white vars.) *Sanguinaria canadensis; Silene alpestris; Statice Armeria alba* (Thrift); *Tiarella cordifolia; Veronica rupestris alba; Vinca minor alba; Viola cornuta alba.*

Summer-flowering: Anemone sylvestris; Campanula carpatica alba; Delphinium chinense album; Dianthus Her Majesty, *D.* Mrs. Sinkins, *D.* Bristol Purity; *Erigeron Coulteri; Galium boreale; Helianthemum,* white vars.; *Heuchera* Perry White; *Lychnis Viscaria alba; Nierembergia rivularis; Oenothera caespitosa; Phlox* Tapis Blanc, *P.* Mia Ruys; *Primula japonica alba; Scabiosa caucasica alba; Sedum album; Stokesia laevis alba; Thymus Serpyllum albus; Tunica Saxifraga alba.*

Autumn-flowering: Aster ericoides; A. ptarmicoides; Chrysanthemum arcticum; Helleborus niger.

[244]

A White Garden in Wales

Annuals for Summer-Flowering
(Only white-flowered forms of kinds named are intended)

Ageratum; *Alyssum maritimum;* Antirrhinum, tall and dwarf; *Argemone mexicana;* Asters, tall and dwarf; Balsam; Bellis; Candytuft; Sweet Sultan; Cornflower, double; Clarkia; Cosmos, early and late; Chinese Pinks; Godetia Duchess of Albany; *Gypsophila elegans;* Heliotrope White Queen; *Lavatera splendens;* Larkspur; Lobelia; Mignonette; *Nicotiana affinis; Omphalodes linifolia;* Pansies; Petunia, double and single; *Phlox Drummondii;* Poppies; Scabiosa Shasta; Sweet Peas; Stocks; Verbena; Zinnias, tall and dwarf.

Spring- and Summer-Flowering Bulbs to Be Planted in Autumn

Allium neapolitanum, A. ursinum; Anthericum Liliago (summer); *Camassia Leichtlinii alba; Chionodoxa Luciliae alba; Colchicum autumnale album, C. speciosum album* (autumn); *Crocus biflorus, C. versicolor picturatus;* hybrid Crocuses (spring-flowering); *C. hadriaticus, C. speciosus albus* (autumn-flowering); *Eremurus Elwesii albus,* 10–12 ft.; *Erythronium californicum, E. giganteum; Fritillaria meleagris alba;* Galanthus (Snowdrop) species; Hyacinths, double and single; *Hyacinthus amethystinus albus; Leucojum aestivum, L. vernum; Lilium auratum* (summer), *L. Brownii* (early summer), *L. candidum, L. Martagon album; L. speciosum album* (late summer), *L. regale* (July); Narcissus, many vars.; *Ornithogalum umbel-*

latum; Tulips, many vars.; *Scilla campanulata alba, S. nutans alba, S. sibirica alba.*

Summer-Flowering Bulbs and Roots
to Be Planted in Spring

Dahlias, tall and dwarf; Gladioli; *Hyacinthus candicans;* Tuberoses, double and single; *Zephyranthes alba.*

Climbers

Actinidia arguta; Clematis Duchess of Edinburgh, *C. Henryi, C. montana, C. paniculata, C. Veitchiana; Ipomoea grandiflora* (Moonflower); *Lonicera Halliana; Lathyrus latifolius albus; Polygonum Auberti;* Rose, many vars.; *Wisteria sinensis alba.*

INDEX

Index

[248]

Index

Index

Index

Index

Index

MacSelf, A. J., 208
Magnolia, 207; *stellata*, 21, 23, 36, 241; *conspicua*, 241
Mallow, Marsh, 147; Musk, 150, 151, 154, 178, 186; Prairie, 151; Greek, 151; Curled, 152; French, 152; Tree, 153; Poppy, 153; Flame, 154
Malope grandiflora, 152
Malus, floribunda, 39; *baccata*, 241
Malva, 147; *moschata*, 150, 186; *m. alba*, 178, 219; *Alcea*, 150; *crispa*, 152
Malvastrum coccineum, 153, 154
Marguerite, 84, 88
Marigold, 79; Marsh, 28
Mazus pumilio, 92
Meadowrue, 139–142, 146, 178; Early, 145
Megapterium missouriensis, 136
Melandryum Elizabethae, 129
Mertensia, 23, 34, 39, 40, 223; *virginica*, 39; *lanceolata*, 40; *ciliata*, 40; *pratensis*, 40
Micromeria, 120
Mignonette, 245
Milne, A. A., 32
Mock Orange, 24
"Modern Herbal, A," 30
Monarda fistulosa alba, 243
Moneywort, 90
Moonflower, 246
Morgan, Cleveland, 180
Muehlenbeckia nana, 120
Mullein, 188–191, 193, 194, 195, 219; Moth, 190; Olympic, 191; Miss Willmott, 193
Muscari, 35, 37; *azureum*, 34; *amethystinum*, 35; *botryoides*, 37; Heavenly Blue, 37; *conicum*, 37; *Argaei*, 37; *armeniacum*, 37; *micranthum*, 37; *neglectum*, 37; Black, 37; *paradoxum*, 37; *racemosum*, 37; *Heldreichi*, 37
"My Garden in Spring," 16, 26
Myosotis, 244; *dissitiflora*, 40; Victoria, 40; White Lady, 40; *sylvatica*, 40; *palustris grandiflora*, 40; *palustris semperflorens*, 40; Ruth

Fisher, 41; Star of Love, 41; *rupicola*, 41; *alpestris*, 41; Blue Beauty, 41
Myrtle, Sand, 118

"Names of Herbs," 197
Narcissus, 21, 245; Poetaz, 22; Poet's, 24, 40
"National Horticultural Magazine," 209
"Natural Rock Gardening," 3
Nepeta Mussini, 217
"New Manual of Botany," 27
Nicotiana affinis, 245
Nierembergia rivularis, 244

Oenothera, 130, 131, 137; *acaulis*, 132; *taraxacifolia*, 132; *aurea*, 132; *biennis*, 132; *b. grandiflora*, 133; *Lamarckiana*, 133; Afterglow, 133; *brachycarpa*, 133; *caespitosa*, 133, 134, 135, 244; *marginata*, 134, 135; *eximia*, 134, 135; *Clutei*, 135; *fruticosa*, 135, 136; *f. major*, 135; *f. Youngii*, 135; *glauca*, 135, 136; *g. Fraseri*, 135; *g. Eldorado*, 135, 136; *missouriensis*, 136; *macrocarpa*, 136; *pumila*, 136; *speciosa*, 137, 243; *s. rosea*, 137; *s. rubra*, 137; *tetraptera*, 137; *Childsii*, 137; *Sarazinii*, 137; *trichocalyx*, 138
Omphalodes, verna, 41; *cappadocica*, 41; *linifolia*, 245
Onagra, biennis, 132; *trichocalyx*, 138
Onion, 72; Allegheny, 73; Prairie, 73
Ornithogalum umbellatum, 245

Pachistima Canbyi, 120
Pachylophus caespitosa, 133
Paeonia, 243
Pansy, 21–24; 245
Papaver, rupifragum, 67; *orientale* Perry's White, 243
Parkinson, John, 104, 132, 148, 152, 225
Pea, Sweet, 237, 239, 247

[253]

Index

Peach, 241; double-flowering, 23
Pella Mountain, 102
Pentstemon, barbatus, 219; *digitalis alba,* 243
Periwinkle, 41
Petrophytum caespitosum, 109
Petunia, 239, 245
Philadelphus, 241
Phlox, 64, 148, 215, 219, 239; *subulata,* 55; *s.* G. F. Wilson, 22, 24; *s. Nelsonii,* 24, 244; Creeping, 37, 98; *stolonifera,* 98; Miss Lingard, 219, 243; *Drummondii,* 239, 245; Jeanne d'Arc, 243; Frau Anton Buchner, 243; Fräulein von Lassburg, 243; Mrs. Jenkins, 243; *divaricata alba,* 244; Tapis Blanc, 244; Mia Ruys, 244
Physostegia, virginica, 186; *v. alba,* 243
Picea, glauca albertiana, 120; *excelsa nana,* 120; *excelsa Gregoryana,* 120; *excelsa Maxwellii,* 120; *excelsa pygmaea,* 120
Pieris, floribunda, 241; *japonica,* 241
Pilewort, 25
Pink, 122, 235; Maiden, 93; American Wild, 122; Peat, 122; Fire, 123; Mullein, 194; Chinese, 245
Pinus, montana, 120; *Mugo,* 120
"Plants from Seed," 208
Platycodon grandiflora album, 243
Pliny, 31
Plum, Beach, 241
Polemonium, 34; *caeruleum,* 39; *c. album,* 243; *reptans,* 39; *pulcherrimum,* 39
Polyanthus, 41
Polygonum Auberti, 246
Poppy, 245; alpine, 68; Celandine, 31; California, 239
Potentilla fruticosa, 120
Pratt, Anne, 226
Primrose, 24, 41; Evening, 130, 131, 138; White Chilean, 132; Common Evening, 132; Tufted, 133; Cowboy, 133; Desert, 138
Primula polyantha, 244
Prunus, tomentosa, 23, 241; *glandulosa sinensis,* 241; *maritima,* 241; *Persica flore-alboplena,* 241
Pulmonaria angustifolia, 38, 223
Purdy, Carl, 125
Pussy Willow, 13, 22
Pyrethrum, 79, 215, 217
Pyrus, baccata, 241; *Sargentii,* 241; *toringoides,* 241

Quaker Lady, 34
Quince, Japanese, 23

Ranunculus, ficaria, 26; *grandiflora,* 29
Rea, John, 224, 225
Rhododendron, 119; *ferrugineum,* 119; *racemosum,* 119; *canadense,* 119; *viscosum,* 242; *carolinianum album,* 241
Rhodora canadense, 119
Rhodotypos kerrioides, 119
Robinson, William, 205, 207, 208, 210
Romneya Coulteri, 227
Rosa, Rouletti, 112; *foliolosa alba,* 113; *Lyonii,* 113; *alpina,* 113; *spithamea,* 114; *nitida,* 114, 158, 159; *arkansana,* 114, 158; *setigera,* 157; *blanda,* 158; *lucida,* 159; *humilis,* 159; *Eglanteria,* 159; *canina,* 160; *Hugonis,* 160; *Xanthina,* 160; *Harisonii,* 161; *Ecae,* 161; *spinosissima,* 161, 242; *altaica,* 161; *Helenae,* 161; *Moyesii,* 162; *Sweginzowi,* 162; *omeiensis,* 162; *Willmottiae,* 162; *setipoda,* 162; *rubrifolia,* 163; *multiflora,* 164; *laevigata,* 164; *bracteata,* 164; *rugosa,* 164; *r. alba,* 242; *multiflora japonica,* 242
Rose, 112, 246; Safrano, 20; Texas, 113; Wild, 155, 156, 157, 163; Prairie, 157; Baltimore Belle, 158; Meadow, 158; Early Wild, 158; Arkansas, 158; Northeastern Pasture, 159; Swamp, 159; Carolina, 159; Dog, 160; Persian Yellow, 161; Scotch, 161; Burnet,

Index

Index

Index

Index

Index

ABOUT THE AUTHOR

Born in Baltimore, Maryland, in 1878, Louise Beebe Wilder was educated privately by tutors. In 1904 she married an architect, Walter Robb Wilder, who designed a house called Balderbrae in Bronxville, New York. Here his wife made her first garden. In 1919 the couple separated and Walter Wilder built a second house nearby, called Little Balderbrae, whose garden was Mrs. Wilder's laboratory and the prime subject of her writings in *House & Garden* and other periodicals and her nine books until her death in 1938.

Elisabeth Sheldon is a regular contributor to *Horticulture* and *Organic Gardening* magazines and is the author of *A Proper Garden*. She lives and gardens in the Finger Lakes area of New York.